Tom Ryalls

Tom is an award-winning writer and cultural organiser, interested in the politics of imagination, and who gets to imagine the future.

He has written work for theatres across the country including HOME in Manchester, Stratford East, the Barbican, Shoreditch Town Hall, the Royal Court Theatre, and Cast in Doncaster. These shows have often tried to grapple with those structures that limit our imagination, and try to centre working-class, disabled and queer imaginations.

He created *The Black Hole* project, a series of shows exploring how art might engage with epilepsy. The first show, *Can You See into a Black Hole?*, was originally commissioned for Shoreditch Town Hall, and eventually redeveloped with Arts Council England funding to tour nationally and to Camden People's Theatre, London. This production then went on to be performed outdoors in Covent Garden, published, and adapted as an audio play by Cast. The second part of the trilogy is for young people and began development with a residency at ArtsDepot.

Tom's work as a cultural organiser has mainly focused on wealth redistribution, and fundraising for projects and organisations that are changing who gets to imagine the future. He has previously been a Head of Development, an Executive Director, and an Arts Fundraising and Philanthropy Fellow with Cause4. He has worked a lot in disability arts practice and is now a founding trustee of Unlimited, a member of the London Area Council of ACE, and the Deputy Chair of their Disability Advisory Committee.

In 2024, his work was celebrated when he was named as one of the ten most influential people in UK performing arts, television and radio on The Shaw Trust's Disability Power 100 list, and in 2025 he became a Clore Fellow and the Chair of Graeae Theatre Company.

**More books about wellbeing for creatives
from Nick Hern Books**

An Actor's Alphabet
*An A to Z of Some Stuff I've Learnt
and Some Stuff I'm Still Learning*
Julie Hesmondhalgh

An Attitude for Acting
How to Survive (and Thrive) as an Actor
Andrew Tidmarsh and Tara Swart

Developing Your Emotional Health
The Compact Guide
Andy Barker, Brian Cooley & Beth Wood

The Dyslexic Actor's Toolkit
Strategies for Success in Your Craft and Career
Deborah Groves

The Golden Rules of Acting
and **More Golden Rules of Acting**
Andy Nyman

The Jobbing Actor
A Coaching Programme for Actors
Letty Butler & Anita Gilbert

Discover more at
www.nickhernbooks.co.uk

THIS BOOK IS SHORT

A Toolkit for Creative ADHDers

Tom Ryalls

NICK HERN BOOKS

London

www.nickhernbooks.co.uk

A Nick Hern Book

This Book is Short: A Toolkit for Creative ADHDers
first published in Great Britain in 2026
by Nick Hern Books Limited,
The Glasshouse, 49a Goldhawk Road,
London W12 8QP

Designed and typeset by Nick Hern Books
Printed in the UK by SRP Ltd, Exeter

A CIP catalogue record for this book is available
from the British Library

ISBN 978 1 83904 434 2

www.nickhernbooks.eo.uk/environmental-policy

Nick Hern Books' authorised representative in the EU is
Easy Access System Europe -Mustamae tee 50, 10621 Tallinn, Estonia
email gpsr.requests@easproject.com

*To all the people who said I wouldn't finish.
How does it feel to be wrong?*

Contents

Introduction

a. Who is this book for?

1. People who have been diagnosed with Attention Deficit Hyperactivity Disorder (ADHD).

2. People who think they have ADHD, but haven't been able to access diagnosis because of the challenges involved in that.

3. People who might have ADHD, but haven't chosen to seek diagnosis because it is not important to them.

4. People who have a creative practice – this might be for a job or as a hobby. My experience is mainly in theatre, but I did the research with lots of different people, so it should apply elsewhere too.

5. Anyone who works with/cares for/spends time with the people above, and who wants to better understand ways they can be more helpful.

6. Anyone else who sometimes feels overwhelmed by the information out there and needs something to guide them.

b. Ways to read this book

1. Don't read it. You don't have to read it if you don't want to. The earth will not stop turning if you don't read it.

2. Look at the contents, choose the sections that look interesting, read those.

3.   Dip into the bits that are useful.

4.   Ignore the bits that aren't useful.

5.   You can read it cover to cover.

6.   You can read it cover to cover but backwards.

7.   Read it while on holiday in Cyprus.

8.   Despite doing a degree in English about ten years ago, I'm not great at reading. I love reading, but unless I get totally absorbed and finish a book in a day, it usually sits on my bedside table half-finished for about two months. So, feel free to leave this book on your bedside table and come back to it in a few years.

9.   Read it in whatever way is useful to you – there is no reward or punishment for reading it in an unexpected order.

c. Things this book is

1.   A toolkit.

2.   A diary.

3.   An attempt to make sense of all the things people have told me about my brain.

d. Things this book is not

1.   A solution to all your problems.

2.   (Possibly) a solution to any of them.

3.   A route to bliss and perfection.

4.   A diagnosis tool.

5.   A form of meditation.

6. Something that will make you cleverer for reading it.

7. Going to tell you that ADHD is a superpower. I think it's patronising to think that people with ADHD, or any neurodivergence/disability must be a superhero. It's othering and we should also have the right to be quite boring and unexceptional.

8. Something you should hoard, please share it.

e. The parts of this book

1. The Creative in Your Own Head. This is the bit about your creative practice, including techniques that might be useful to finish your own creative project.

2. The Creative in the Sector. The thing is, sometimes you can't use those techniques because of the requirements the creative sector puts on us. This section is about how we might deal with that, from networking to applying for funding.

3. The Creative in the World. We exist in this liberal-ish bubble of the arts, but we often go outside of it for our day jobs or because it's not our entire life. This section is about those bigger things like medication, how to find a good 'survival job', how to get help at work, and advocating for yourself in your personal networks.

f. Ways information is organised in each part

1. Each part has an introduction with some context.

2. Then each part is broken down into topics and sometimes subtopics, so you can more easily identify what you need.

3. At the end of each topic there is a **'TL;DR' section** (i.e. Too Long; Didn't Read), which summarises that technique in a short sentence in case you want to skip the context.

4. Every so often, when there is a collection of useful techniques there is a **'Flick Page'**, which is a one-page reference guide you can download from www.nickhernbooks.co.uk/this-book-is-short and print. These pages contain the key reminders for when you're experiencing a specific problem.

g. Words and phrases that might be new to you

1. Neurotypical – This is a word used to describe people that have a typical neurological function, or whose brains work in a typical way.

2. Neurodivergent – This word describes a person or brain which diverges from how we think brains typically work. It is an imperfect term, and we shouldn't constantly compare ourselves to what is typical. It is often used to describe ADHD, Autism, Dyslexia, Dyspraxia, Dyscalculia, amongst other things.

3. Neurodiverse – A group of people where there is a mix of neurotypical and/or different neurodivergences are neurodiverse.

4. Emotional Dysregulation – This is where a person experiences emotions in a way that might not be considered typical. It often involves feeling overwhelmed.

5. Masking – This normally happens when a neurodivergent person is trying to seem more neurotypical. It is like wearing a mask to appear neurotypical. For example, when I hide my fidgets under a table in meetings so it looks more like I am sitting still.

6. Othering – This is the act of making someone feel different, or highlighting their difference so they feel 'other' as opposed to 'same/similar'. For example, constantly saying that someone with ADHD is stupid because they can't finish their work. It makes them feel like they don't fit in.

This all started when I was eight. I went on a camping trip to a place called Wetwang (it's real) and had my first epileptic seizure – but that's the subject of a play I wrote, so no spoilers here. This event came to define most of my medical history. The medical urgency of my seizures meant that most other physical or psychological care needs became second to this.

Something slightly odd that might be related to my brain, like constant daydreaming, was often explained away with epilepsy. It wasn't until I was volunteering in a community garden in my mid-twenties, that someone said to me that if I were a kid they would send me for an ADHD assessment. After years of explaining everything away with epilepsy, there was finally a spark of curiosity.

At first I thought it was unlikely, I had done quite well in school and I didn't really fit any of the stereotypes I had been fed about ADHD growing up. But there is nothing better to me than a distraction, so off I went and did a lot of research.

Within a few months I was using techniques I had found in ADHD management books and podcasts – they were useful, but I felt like a fraud. These techniques felt like they weren't meant for me. This is what spurred me on to explore diagnosis, but a voice in the back of my head was still saying it might just be my quirky epileptic brain.

A doctor gave me a diagnosis letter, and as I told people it suddenly clicked into place. The letter gave people permission to see through this cloud of epileptic mystery that had surrounded my brain, and friends and family very suddenly realised why I was like I was.

Though it wasn't so clear for me. What was I supposed to do now? I had my eyes opened to a whole world of information about how my brain worked and I immediately shut them because it felt overwhelming.

By this point it was around 2018, I had made a few pieces of fringe theatre, nothing that lasted more than an hour or demanded particularly complex resources. I was starting to write bigger shows, the kind of scripts that would require me to focus on them for over a year in massive detail. I had to meet deadlines that were important and that had more substantial fees attached to them.

I knew that I had four unfinished scripts in a drawer, because after three months I normally get distracted by another idea and start to write something new without finishing the previous thing. I had no idea how I was going to finish bigger shows.

ADHD is not the stereotype of young boys being unruly in a classroom; it manifests in different ways for different people, and often interacts with other aspects of our lives, our health, and the ways in which we are marginalised. For creatives, it can look like struggling to remain focused while performing a show, missing deadlines or auditions, getting distracted when you're supposed to be learning your lines or working on something. It can often escalate into late nights trying to catch up on the things you haven't done, which makes you tired the next day, which in turn makes everything worse, and you drop further behind. It can become an endless void of repetitive failure, which you are determined to resolve, but your brain won't always cooperate.

It was in one of these late-night cycles that I found a helpful way of framing what I was trying to understand. It is often said that ADHD is the inability to focus, but the most helpful metaphor I have found to describe a lot of ADHD is to think we have *too much* focus. We are trying to focus on all things at once, and we're not great at prioritising those things, so we either jump between tasks or are entirely paralysed because we can't imagine a route through doing everything at once.

I needed to take all of the things I could possibly focus on and narrow them down to be able to look at them. After years of mystery and distraction, it was about time I took the chaos of my brain and sorted through it.

That's where this book begins. I applied for a grant from Arts Council England called 'Developing Your Creative Practice' in order to spend some time researching how to be a writer with ADHD. As part of that process I kept a diary as I began to grapple with my brain, and I've brought all those notes together for this first part.

1.1. I can't get started

1.1.1. Do a 'shit draft'

Sat behind a laptop late at night, when all good ADHD ideas begin – I ignored the keyboard and screen and started picking my nails.

A lot of people who are diagnosed with ADHD as an adult have developed coping mechanisms, which can manifest in lots of ways. My most gross coping mechanism is that I pick my nails so that I don't fidget and I can sit still. I subconsciously learned to redirect the fidget to something nobody would notice, unless you try to give me a manicure or check my cuticles.

It felt easier to start my research by looking at the things I already knew about myself, and I knew I couldn't imagine writing a script without a 'shit draft'.

I can write really quickly, but only after I've written the first draft of a script. Starting a new project, sitting down and focusing on a blank piece of paper – and trying to fill it – is hard. My brain is often trying to focus on all the possible ways that a story can go, and it's so overwhelming that I can't narrow it down to one I can write on a piece of paper.

I can't remember why I started doing this, but I think I have lied to every person who has ever read a 'draft one' of a script I've written.

I set myself a ridiculous time limit, normally it's something like a day. I lock myself away somewhere, and I attempt to write the worst version of the script possible in that time. Sometimes whole scenes are just a list of actions and things that need to change in order to get me to the next scene. The dialogue is really 'on the nose', most of the characters are swearing at someone else to create conflict, and the ending often makes me cringe when I read it back.

In the shit draft of one show I wrote, there was a dog who had lines. I imagine that a dog had walked past the window of wherever I was writing, I got distracted, and it immediately ended up in my script. This didn't come to fruition; it turns out it's quite difficult to get dogs to speak.

I found other creatives do the same. I know a lot of ADHD actors who prefer to improvise their way through a script before learning lines, or designers who just stick whatever is lying around their house to a board as a first draft of a set design. The principle can be applied to whatever your role or your process is.

Your aim with your shit draft is to make it as bad as possible, because then you're not trying to pick one good version of the project to focus on. You're allowing yourself to wander through your distractions and explore lots of possibilities at once.

The key components of the shit draft are:

1. *Intention* – You have to plan to make it the worst version possible, so you don't begin to question yourself.

2. *Time* – The short time frame is important too, because it creates a sense of crisis that forces you to get things done and not spend too much time getting lost in detail.

3. *Forwards* – You cannot go backwards. You must keep moving forwards, even if that means sacrificing quality or even basic sense in this draft.

From this point, you've started the script, you've done the hard part. Continuing from here is much easier. Instead of looking at a blank page with millions of possible options that overwhelm you, you're looking at a lot of choices you've already made.

For the next draft, you can narrow down on smaller sections and begin to work on them more effectively, because some options have already been discounted. It's much less overwhelming. The next draft is my real draft one, where I've spent time to craft something.

TL;DR: Set yourself a short time frame, and do the worst version of the task possible, so you're technically redrafting from there.

1.1.2. Subtask it

Having found one technique that helped me to get started, there was definitely a part of my brain that thought I was done. I had succeeded in something; my brain was happy – I wanted to be distracted from looking for new techniques.

So, I did what I had always done when starting a new project: I went to buy a new notebook. Obviously that would give me the motivation to keep going, right? Not true.

There is a pile of notebooks in my room full of half-started to-do lists that I never finished. Usually I lose a notebook for a few months and then it turns up somewhere, but by this point I've moved on, so it goes on the stack. To-do lists have never been my friend, but I did begin to find new ways to use them.

When I look at a to-do list that includes 'Write a play', I don't imagine a linear, manageable trajectory, I imagine myself doing every single part of that writing simultaneously. ADHD brains are not naturally good at prioritising things, or to put it another way, focusing on certain things in a helpful order.

When this happens I don't start the task, because I am so overwhelmed, it's a form of mental paralysis. And I will put off starting to write for as long as possible, so I don't have to imagine the idea of writing a hundred scenes at once.

There is a similar feeling for actors, imagining they must learn every line of a play simultaneously, or for lighting designers imagining they have to be up forty ladders at once, focusing lights.

Before I had language associated with ADHD, I had always called this feeling of being overwhelmed 'anxiety', and I knew when I was anxious I would write a list of all the micro-actions I needed to do to get through the next hour.

I began applying this idea of breaking things down to my to-do list (more on how I stopped losing those lists later). I stopped writing lists that said 'Write a play' and started having a list called 'Write a play' with tasks like 'Do the shit draft of Scene One' or 'Get *x* character out of *y* situation in Scene Seven'.

It sounds simple, but I call it 'subtasking'. It means that instead of looking at a task with a huge number of possible routes, you identify tangible routes that can be completed in manageable chunks.

Instead of:	Do the subtask:
Learn your lines.	Learn page one, learn page two, learn page three...

| Write the play. | Draft Scene One, draft Scene Two, get the main character into trouble... |
| Read the play. | Read Scene One, read Scene Two, read Scene Three... |

Each time you complete one of those tiny tasks, your brain releases some fun chemicals (dopamine) that motivate you to keep going. You get lots of little doses regularly, instead of one big peak occasionally. Chain them together, and the constant subtask completion helps with brain regulation. Instead of going through peaks and troughs where dopamine is high or low, we're trying to manage it back to a constant medium.

People often underestimate the act of naming things. Subtasking is not a new thing; it's something that people will do instinctively, but naming the process makes it something you can actively choose to do, instead of letting it be an intangible thing you might forget to do.

The balance you have to find, and there is no secret to finding this, is making sure the administration of writing the lists doesn't take too much time away from doing the tasks.

TL;DR: Break a to-do list into small manageable tasks called subtasks.

1.1.3. Sessions

I sat down one day to start doing some writing, using my subtasks, and faced a piece of paper with an endless list of subtasks on it. I felt like I had failed, but my instinct told me to push forward, because really what I needed was a way to build a box around certain tasks so that I didn't have to look at the others.

Luckily for me, neurodivergent people tend to gravitate towards each other subconsciously. I had ended up in a small productivity

WhatsApp group (more on this later), where some friends suggested I try the Pomodoro technique. This is where you set a twenty-five-minute timer for your work to create a sense of urgency, and then time a five-minute break for non-work distractions.

There is something about twenty-five minutes that has never fitted very well with my brain. I can't handle anything that doesn't neatly fit into a clock face; in the morning I will only set an alarm if the time is in a unit of fifteen minutes from the hour.

However, the concept of breaking down time, and naming what those units were, did become something useful. I ended up calling these things 'sessions'. Again, this is not something new, but it felt useful to claim it for myself by giving a name to it.

Instead of knowing I have thirty subtasks to do in a day, I can arrange my day so I have three subtasks to complete within ten sessions of a set length. This means when I start to work, I'm looking at a small list for one session, as opposed to an overwhelming list for the whole day. I don't look at future sessions until I get to them.

Sessions can be any length that is useful to you, and can happen at any time. They can be very short or very long, based on what your brain needs. They should be timed, to give them a definite start and end point, with an alarm clearly alerting you when time's up.

I think of this as mimicking what some people do more subconsciously. My brain doesn't subconsciously sort a task out into its smaller components and then arrange it neatly in time, so I have to make myself do that intentionally.

You also need to time the rest gaps between the sessions, or you might find yourself doing laundry for twenty minutes and forgetting about the things you were supposed to be doing.

TL;DR: Break your day up into sessions, and assign subtasks to each session, so the day feels more manageable.

1.1.4. Leave yourself a gift

Back to a morning sat in front of a laptop, I arrange the subtasks into sessions and still I am a bit stuck. Once I get going I know it will be fine, because I know I have a structure that will carry me through. But taking that first step in a morning is hard.

Instead of writing, I searched for a distraction and found it on Twitter (now X). Even though I remember the existence of the tweet, I have never been able to find the actual tweet again, and I just remember it was something about productivity.

It was one of many momentary distractions that didn't hold my attention long enough to cement properly in my brain, but it did change something in me. It suggested that writers should start their day with an easy task.

This was my problem, I had set that first tiny threshold a little too high for myself and so it felt bigger than it actually was. So I began experimenting with how to lower the threshold.

Inspired by that tweet, I settled on trying to leave an easy start for myself. When you finish the last sessions of a day, plan for the first sessions of a future day, and leave yourself a gift. This means that you should leave yourself an easily completable single task – such as 'Finish three lines of Scene Seven' – that can be done in a very short session – fifteen minutes or less – at the beginning of the next creative work day.

There is nothing I find more challenging than working for hours until I manage to tick something off my to-do list; the time stretches on until I lapse into daydreams. So starting your day with a feeling of completing a task gives you that brief hit of dopamine and encourages you to continue. It's like getting caffeine from your morning coffee, it gives you a little bit of fuel to get going.

It is also important for me that you assign one task for one session, because it creates such a strong sense of achievement that way.

I often plan a short break in between sessions, but I rarely end up wanting to take it after the first session; the satisfaction of ticking something off the list quickly makes me want to continue into other tasks.

This is where ADHD began to make more sense to me. There are a few different descriptions of ADHD, but the most useful one for me says that our brains have fluctuations of dopamine more than other brains. When it's high we are inattentive because we avoid stimulation, we want to bring it down. When it's low, we are hyperactive and crave stimulation to raise it. This is a very simple reduction and paraphrasing, but I have found it a useful broad idea to identify what is happening to me at any given moment.

Most humans have some kind of fluctuation, but they can be more pronounced in someone with ADHD. The techniques I was gathering were about reclaiming some influence over those peaks and troughs. Instead of doing huge tasks and starting the day with a huge peak, I was completing something easy and simple to create a small blip. I was trying to avoid the extremes, and it was beginning to work.

TL;DR: Leave yourself one subtask that can be completed in a single short session at the beginning of your day.

1.1.5. The task/session matrix

I had so far gathered four techniques I could use to help get projects started. I came back to my laptop and I tried to use them, and stopped immediately because I was getting overwhelmed at which one to use. It's great to have options, but I had created the opposite effect and given myself too many options.

This is often the challenge with ADHD – we need to put structures in place to help manage our experience of the world, but it takes some executive functioning to use those techniques in the first place. I needed a way to bring these things together, so I didn't have to organise the techniques before I could use them.

My thought process often isn't particularly linear, I tend to jump around a lot. This means I often resist writing things in large chunks of text where thoughts have to be arranged in a neat order. This probably explains why this book is a selection of small sections. I find it easier to break up information and arrange it visually so I tried to apply this to my new techniques.

I tried drawing the techniques as a diagram or a table. It was a good distraction and something to do with my fidgety hands – and it turned out to be quite useful.

	Session 1 10:00 – 10:15	Session 2 10:30 – 11:15	Session 3 11:20 – 12:00
Task 1	A 'gift' subtask	Subtask 1 Subtask 2 Subtask 3	
Task 2		Subtask 1	Subtask 2 Subtask 3

This table allowed me to contain all the techniques:

- I am planning sessions along the top, and I know the first session is always short.

- The first note on the template was to leave a 'gift' for the next working day.

- The second note was 'Does this need a shit draft?'

- I try to finish a session by starting the first element of the next task. As you can see, I am doing subtask 1 of task 2 at the end of session 2.

The sum total of all this exploration of the subconscious coping mechanisms I had created to try and make it easier to start tasks was the task-session matrix. You don't need to use that name, but it does turn the act of drawing a table on some paper into something more exciting, as if Doctor Who might be about to turn up and help me write this play.

I turned the template into a table and sometimes started to prepare it the night before, so when I started in the morning, my day was laid out in a way that felt easier to engage with. All the techniques I had developed were contained in the table, so when I looked at my day it didn't feel like an overwhelming mess – it felt like a small and achievable task I could do to get started without trying to hold the rest in my brain. You can also physically cover the later sections so your mind doesn't wonder about them and start getting overwhelmed at the amount that needs to be done.

This is something I have generally found useful with ADHD: the more I can get out of my brain, the less overwhelmed I feel.

It's an incredibly simple table, and it might be that another format works better for you. The important part of it was that I had made a system that worked for me. I know I like to organise things visually, so that was the format I chose.

TL;DR: Whatever your collection of techniques are, bring them together into a system which can allow you to start a task. This should be something on one page, which has everything you need.

Techniques you could use	Questions to ask yourself
1.1.1. Do a shit draft 1.1.2. Subtask it 1.1.3. Sessions 1.1.4. Leave yourself a gift 1.1.5. The task/session matrix	• What task could you do right now? • Could you do a 'shit version' of the task? • Would a timer and some urgency help? • Could you leave yourself a gift for next time? • Could you break this task down?

	Session 1: (Leave yourself a gift)	Session 2:	Session 3:	Session 4:	Session 5:
Task 1:					
Task 2:					
Task 3:					

1.2. I can't keep going

1.2.1. Body doubling/accountability

I started my research by learning about how I like to start things, which did feel a bit like cheating at the time, because it felt like procrastinating from starting. Now I had started, I had to figure out how to keep going beyond having created one little table I could fill in.

That's the challenge with ADHD: even if you start, it can take a lot of effort to keep going. Who's going to notice if I don't get a task all the way to the end? I am probably going to get distracted before I notice, and then suddenly the deadline is in three minutes and I haven't done anything at all.

This is where I started talking to other people with ADHD, instead of reading books and articles, because that had become boring. I figured that if I scheduled to have coffee with people to ask them about their experiences, it would at least mean I was contributing something to my research. This stray thought then became the basis of an entire support system.

Have you ever felt that you are more productive in a coffee shop than in your own flat? Or preferred to work with a friend as opposed to sitting somewhere alone? Or gone to the trouble of having coffee with twenty artists to talk about an idea instead of reading a book about that idea? I had spent a lot of my life preferring to do things with other people in the room instead of locking myself away to do things alone. I had thought this was just the collaborative way I approached things. But it was my friend Jen that gave me a name for this: body doubling.

Self-accountability doesn't seem to be our strength, as much as we want to just get things done, there are no real consequences other than our own frustration if we're holding ourselves accountable.

Wherever possible with ADHD, I found it useful to externalise accountability.

Luckily, those conversations I was having gave me an explanation for this. The reason why a coffee shop can feel more effective is because people are observing you, and you begin to wonder if they notice if you don't do the things you said you would do – and that judgement holds you accountable.

It gets even more effective if you tell people what you're planning on doing. Suddenly someone notices if you're daydreaming out the window, and even if they don't say anything, you have been noticed. The act of someone else noticing your intentions means you're not the only one holding yourself accountable.

I really began to notice this idea when I realised the most effective way to get me to do the vacuuming was if my housemates sat in the same room while I did it. I am not the kind of human that is designed to live alone, it would be chaos.

At first I started asking a friend to come and sit in a coffee shop and work with me; they didn't need to do anything, we would just write in the same space. But it's expensive to go out for coffee all the time, so I began to boil it down to its bare bones as a money-saving exercise.

Then I joined a WhatsApp group with some other creatives, and we began co-working across different disciplines. I love writing when there's background noise, so I love it if an actor wants to be in the same room learning lines while I write. A friend who is a set designer often doubles with a composer, because they like to hear fragments of music while they work. You can define the right conditions for you, and it often takes a bit of experimentation.

The three basic steps of body doubling for me are:

1.　Tell someone what you need to achieve.

2.　Give them a time frame for when they should check in on you.

3. Ask them to observe you in some way, whether this is in person, online, or via messaging. They don't need to watch you all of the time – being in the same room is fine.

Ways you might achieve this are:

1. Create a WhatsApp group with some friends, and check in at the start of a work day about what you want to achieve and set times when you'll check in on progress. There is also an online timer called Cuckoo where you can share a link remotely and see the same countdown timer.

2. Work in a public space where people can observe you working; it's more effective if other people know what you need to do but not entirely necessary.

3. If you're working with an organisation, ask them if they can kindly and without too much pressure let you work in their building and ask someone to body double on the tasks.

4. If you have a script to write, agree with a friend that you'll share it with them, no matter the progress, at regular intervals. This can be applied to taking notes, building a sculpture, designing a set. Send a progress report to someone – they don't need to give you feedback, they just need to acknowledge it and create that accountability.

5. There are online groups you can join where people sit on video-calling platforms, share their task lists, and work together while holding each other accountable.

Body doubling is really effective for me, and can be used for the non-creative elements of what we do as well. Now, I do two structured sessions per week where I go through a list of quite boring admin tasks I hate doing, but I do them in a body-doubling session and talk about what I'm doing as I do it. This creates accountability around the less exciting elements of what I do, and it means emails don't go unanswered for two months.

TL;DR: Don't work alone. Set your subtasks, tell someone else what they are, and work together/on a call/in a messaging group to hold each other accountable.

1.2.2. Micro-deadlines

Sometimes it's not practical to be in a specific space with another person; sometimes people are sick and can't be there or have a last-minute change of plans. This means we need to find alternatives.

I built on my point in the previous section about sending script drafts to a friend, and realised it's also possible to push body doubling to a more specific place. If you can't find a way for someone to observe the process of you working, you might find a way for someone to observe the products you create from that process.

I am generally quite uncomfortable with deadlines, and I have a history of missing them. Though I do think this is largely because people set me huge deadlines where I need to finish a big task, like a script, in the next year. That huge deadline doesn't quite work for my brain, and it still gets done at the last minute.

However, the more I started sending drafts of my work to a friend, the more I realised how useful it was. I was doing this out of choice and I began to experiment with what would happen if I set schedules to these emails. This created deadlines, but they were micro-deadlines that I had chosen.

The friend didn't need to check it, or judge it, they just needed to acknowledge it. Knowing that someone was observing the product of my progress created a similar feeling of accountability around me.

This book is a good example of how I have used this technique. I calculated how many words I would have to write to hit my deadlines on time, and then I scheduled micro-deadlines every week (except when I was on holiday) that I had to hit. Every week on Friday I show my word count to a colleague to show them how much progress I've made. That person has never commented on the work or judged me, they just acknowledge the amount of words.

There is a useful accountability in knowing that on Friday I'm going to have to tell someone if I'm behind.

Micro-deadlines and body doubling can feel like I'm advocating for shame as a tool to manage ADHD, but that's not my intention. Your mum visiting your flat and judgementally commenting on its cleanliness while you clean is a form of body doubling, but it's not a healthy one.

It's important that your body double is a person you trust, and that you know will not assign any kind of value judgement to your progress. The aim is not to make you worry constantly about hitting your goal; it's to remind you when you get distracted that someone else is helping you keep on track too.

We should be setting our own micro-deadlines so that we own them, so that they are not externally imposed, but just externally held. The person acting in solidarity with you should not be passing any judgement or assigning any kind of value to the work you are doing. It is not their job to say whether it is good.

Guilt and shame were features of the subconscious coping mechanisms I developed before my diagnosis and awareness; now I think of these techniques more in a solidarity model. In fact, I most often body double and set micro-deadlines with other people who have ADHD, and we do it for each other.

TL;DR: Instead of having one deadline a long way into the future, create progressive micro-deadlines where you are held accountable for making progress.

1.2.3. An iterative process

Breaking down my process into micro-deadlines drew my attention to how much I liked working in small chunks, how it was much easier for me to build a project in small stages instead of disappearing for a year and being expected to form something perfect by the end.

Making art or being creative isn't a linear process, but in a lot of creative sectors, including theatre, there is often a belief that some creatives disappear into a room and some time later this perfectly formed piece of work emerges.

I don't believe that this myth is useful for anyone. I think it comes from many factors, including the challenges in making a lot of art profitable and the scarce resources for creativity, which means we are a little nervous of sharing anything that isn't robust enough to be considered high value.

For creatives with ADHD this can be heightened. I generally write drafts of plays quicker, but I write a higher number of drafts than neurotypical writers I know. This is because I need to develop momentum to get through a draft with some focus, and get it done quickly. I like the pressure. I also don't always pay a lot of attention when writing, if I am always going back and checking things, then I get distracted and go down a rabbit hole. This means my early drafts are not well structured, and have a lot of typos, but I need that to happen in order to see how I want to change it.

My favourite writing process was when I created a show called *Can You See into a Black Hole?* I made a version of the show and it played a few nights in the basement of Shoreditch Town Hall and I got some feedback. I then made the show again a while later, and it ran for a bit longer at Camden People's Theatre and a venue in Leeds that was run by Slung Low – this draft was much better. Then a few years later, I surprisingly got the opportunity to have it performed outdoors in Covent Garden and we created a final version. I was really happy with that final version, because the previous sharings had given me accountability and some good feedback which had helped me keep going and really grapple with the structure of the piece. It allowed me to get distracted with other projects in between, so I didn't spend the whole time feeling frustrated.

As the context around a piece of work changes, the piece of work might need to change. When I was making *Can You See into a Black Hole?*, three days before we opened for the second time, the first images inside a black hole were released. The entire context around the metaphor changed, and so the show continued to evolve.

This is not an uncommon way of thinking about making work in a process for someone that might call themselves a 'theatre-maker' as opposed to a writer. In a more traditional commissioning process for a writer, there is generally an expectation that you are set a deadline and deliver successive drafts which improve at each stage. Then at some point you will reach the point of it being 'finished' and only then will it generally be shared with a significant audience. This more traditional process is what I find difficult.

Other artists with ADHD I chatted to had similar experiences; this iterative way of making things was incredibly useful. In these processes we had found feedback effective, and I think a lot of that is because there was no expectation of the project being 'finished' or implicitly 'good' in any way. It was always understood that the project might continue to change and develop, and there was no fixed point we were working towards where it would reach perfection.

This reframed micro-deadlines for me. They were not restricting me, but actually freeing me to make my process feel more iterative. With micro-deadlines you can plan in time to get distracted by other things until your mind wanders back to the project you're supposed to be doing.

This feels simple, but this curiosity about how I could make my process more iterative continued to be a theme long after this realisation.

TL;DR: Micro-deadlines break down the expectation that you have to go away and make something perfect; in fact, you are iterating something.

1.2.4. Feedback

As I leaned more into thinking of my process as iterative, and drawing on what I had loved about creating *Can You See into a Black Hole?*, I knew I would need to define a way of receiving feedback that didn't demoralise me. Luckily, I had a good sense of how I liked to receive feedback, because I had an informal process already that had been adapted from a process I had learned when I did my degree, which I think was adapted from another process.

For the first time I wrote it down and the rough steps go:

1. Readers/viewers/watchers say what stood out to them.

2. Those same people get to ask questions about things they don't understand.

3. The creator can answer these, or can save them for another time. It is generally recommended that the creator only accepts questions they realise they already have of the piece of work.

4. The creator gets to ask questions of people, and the challenge is that people should not make suggestions. It is the responsibility of the creator to solve problems, and it is the responsibility of the group/person to reveal things the creator might need to see. An example of this might be 'How did you feel in Scene Seven?', as opposed to 'What should I do to improve Scene Seven?'

5. There is then free time where the creator can create rules depending on what they need. Maybe they now feel comfortable with taking direct pointers, maybe they just want to end on some more positive comments.

This is not specifically useful only to people with ADHD – I think it's a useful framework for a lot of people. But it allows work to be shared without 'criticism' which usually aims to point out faults and makes anyone who is sensitive to rejection close up. It also doesn't work on the assumption that there is a mythical place we are all working towards, where the piece of work will be completed. We are not searching for a secret answer that will get us there; we are creating a space where a writer/creator can see their piece more clearly in any one moment.

This feedback process was something I could now communicate to people in order to make sure my work didn't have to exist in isolation, so I could share it at regular intervals. I am not insisting that you use this process, but experiment with what works for you, and define your process so that you can communicate that to people.

It is a myth that feedback should hurt. Feedback should make the work the best version of itself, it should not try and shape the creative project – that is the job of the creatives.

TL;DR: Define your own feedback process, and make sure you communicate it to people.

1.2.5. Game-ification

The next technique I added to my list came from a more unexpected place. I had coffee at Somerset House with the performance artist Victoria Melody in the middle of a heatwave and I talked about how unstimulating I was finding writing. I wasn't enjoying sitting in a room at a desk and trying to get words down on a piece of paper, it felt like the exact opposite of the exciting worlds I was trying to create within my plays.

I had started making theatre because I loved live performance, not because I loved pieces of paper. This book has been harder to write than any play, because it exists primarily on a piece of paper. I think a lot of creatives experience the same thing; we try to make our practice resemble something that seems more like 'work'. If there's a desk involved, then my mum is more likely to understand what I do.

Victoria's terrifying suggestion to this was to stop writing.

Her practice has often been about learning a new skill, or living a new kind of life. She has become a pigeon racer, funeral director and a dog handler. Her enthusiasm for things that other people were enthusiastic about was infectious, and it created shows with absolutely no need for sitting behind a desk for prolonged periods.

Often, we assume we are at fault if we're struggling to engage with work because of our ADHD. We assume that we need a structure to be put in place so we can engage with a perfectly valid process. But what if the process of making the work isn't the right one? What happens when we accept that our brains function as they do, and that the process has to change? What if making art is just boring sometimes?

Victoria had given me a very simple provocation and I began to explore how I might do my practice if I allowed it to be fun for me.

The most common way I get distracted from writing is playing video games. I have often wondered if I should cut out the distraction and write a video game, but it is a world I don't understand well. I began to work out how I could make my process more like a video game. I am sure I'm not the first person to call this 'game-ification'.

At first I would do this in small ways. I tried drafting an entire show using only songs. Each scene had one to three songs that controlled the emotional journey of the scene, and that was fun but I did eventually have to write on top of those songs.

Next, I tried to remove the act of writing, because I can't actually write at the speed my brain thinks, and that creates an endless, frustrating cycle. One thing I do enjoy, and that I do well, is that I can talk very fast. Anyone who has ever sat through a presentation I have given would disagree about it being a good thing, but this is not about them. My mouth can keep up with the speed of my ideas in a way my hands typing can't, and so I discovered speech-to-text software.

Instead of sitting behind a desk, I experimented with writing comedic scenes and stood in a room with a microphone as if I was doing stand-up. I began doing funny little impressions of the characters and swapping voices, and this software would write it down for me. I was producing a script, but I definitely was not writing it. It was so enjoyable, a few times I invited friends to watch and it was really funny.

It also allowed my brain to wander slightly; instead of putting the writing in a very linear fashion, characters would take less formal routes and that would give me new ideas.

Eventually this became *Education, Education, Karaoke*, but that's the focus of Part Two, so no spoilers.

I have found actors with ADHD to be generally pretty terrible at learning lines in a linear way, but really quite incredible at telling a story they've made up on the spot. It doesn't always quite reach an ending, but it's a really exciting journey they are invested in and I become very enthusiastic about their enthusiasm. This is why I often encourage actors to get more involved in improvisation, as well as Shakespeare. Or I suggest they come up with a game like learning lines backwards if they want to learn a more traditional script.

If you use the same game-ification every time, then it might get boring, so you have to find new game-ifications. The important part is not what the process is, but that it's new or unexpected and fun.

Here are some of my favourite game-ifications I have found as I spoke to more artists:

1.   If you normally write a script, speak it.

2.   If you normally make jewellery with your hands, use your feet.

3.   If you normally make extensive character notes when researching a role as an actor, make those notes exclusively through drawing with crayons.

4.   Cut up the lines you need to learn and instead of trying to learn them, jumble them up and try to put them back in an order that makes sense.

Game-ification can be pushed further too: micro-deadlines and subtasks can function as checkpoints in the game where you can get rewards. For every checkpoint you hit – can you do something you're really itching to do?

TL;DR: Sometimes the creative process you are used to is boring, so you might need to change it up and turn it into a game.

1.2.6. Sensory input

I hosted a creative chat with a few other ADHD artists and we talked about our perfect work environment, and the things we needed to do our work well. There was some agreement that we generally found standing desks useful, we generally all liked to use body doubling, but the big disagreement we all had was noise.

ADHDers can be sensitive to noise – really, we can be sensitive to any kind of sensory input. For me it's noise and touch; I get intensely distracted and frustrated at any kind of inconsistent pressure on my body. I'm not ticklish but any kind of tickly feeling, itchy clothes, a loose thread on a T-shirt, and I cannot focus on anything else.

The other artists and I could not agree on the sound we liked to have when we worked, and a big part of this was that what we liked to listen to changed throughout the day. Sometimes with ADHD if you're very focused and stimulated, you really don't want any sound because it is too stimulating. Sometimes, if you're in an inattentive mood, you really want specific sounds that stimulate you in certain ways in order to give you something you enjoy focusing on.

Sometimes if I get too much sensory input, then I feel overwhelmed. I don't often stay at club nights the whole night, even if I enjoy it at first, because eventually my brain finds the noise too much.

Sometimes I don't get enough, and I get irritable and fidgety and I look for other things to do which just leads to more distraction.

There is no simple suggestion, like listening to white noise while working, but it is useful to pay attention to your need or aversion to sensory input and try to work out what kinds of things indicate you need your sensory environment to change. It might be that throughout the day what you want changes, and so it's useful to know what playlists to have or what you might need to put in place so you can meet those needs.

Some kinds of sensory input I use often are:

- Brown noise – which is like white noise but a lot softer. My favourite is a track I have of a microphone that is inside a tumble dryer full of soft blankets. The sound is low and repetitive but not disruptive, so if I need a little extra sensory input while writing I find it useful.

- When I need a lot of sensory input I listen to Cascada, but I also grew up in Doncaster in the '00s so that might be a bit specific to me.

- If I am not craving sound input then sometimes I use smells. I am wary of advocating for scented candles as a management tool, because I think the overpriced market is already making some questionable claims around wellbeing, but they can be useful. Something minty is often just enough to keep me focused.

- Sometimes I want no noise so I have some cheap noise-cancelling headphones I got online. I don't need them to have a lot of features, I just need them to make it quiet. This is normally when I'm really focused because my writing is really stimulating, and I can't handle any more sensory input.

- Sometimes if I am overwhelmed with sensory input, and quiet isn't enough, I find a weighted blanket or something similar is really useful to help me regulate a bit. I can tell when I need this, my laptop screen feels really bright and my eyes usually get quite tired. I don't necessarily need a nap, but I do need to feel calm.

- I struggle if I am too hot or too cold. I permanently carry around a backpack which is mainly full of layering options in case I want to cool down/warm up. I'm also not a fan of sleeves because they make my arms warm; most of my jumpers have stretched elastic around the wrists because I am always rolling them up to my elbows.

I began to find it useful to imagine a scale of sensory input, and I could work out where on the scale I sat and then increase/decrease my sensory input accordingly. This meant I didn't have to use language like 'overwhelmed' which comes with a sense of judgement; I talk about being 'overstimulated' or 'understimulated' instead.

TL;DR: Your level of stimulation will affect the sensory input you want, so prepare the different types you might need to create a useful working environment.

1.2.7. The dump list/distraction box

I try not to use the word 'distraction' with ADHD, because I think it's a word that's at the core of an outdated understanding of ADHD. Distractibility is not all of our experience, it is just a small part of it.

For me the most frustrating part of distractibility is when I have good focus, and I suddenly remember that I need to change the cat's litter, so I go and do that. While I'm getting the litter out I notice I've forgotten to water a plant on the windowsill, so I get the jug out of the cupboard to water the plant. As I'm filling the jug I remember I forgot to call our water supplier about the meter not working so I go back to my laptop to find the phone number. While looking for the number I see an article about how we're running out of water in the climate crisis and suddenly I'm looking up ways to stop the world burning.

Forty-five minutes later, I have hyperfocused on climate justice and I am absolutely prepared for questions on the water cycle at the next pub quiz. But I have not completed any of the tasks I set myself, and entirely forgotten the day started with me writing. I get increasingly angry at myself but still can't go back to working because changing the cat's litter feels so urgent.

You can replace these tasks with other things, but I found a version of it was a common experience for a lot of the ADHD creatives I spoke to. The best solution I found was from a theatre director, who would have a wall in any rehearsal room where actors could add a thought about their character that they didn't want to pursue now, but might pursue later. It can be really useful to wander down random avenues as an actor and explore surprising choices, but it can also be very disorientating if you are not able to pursue one avenue of thought for long enough.

This distraction wall allows actors to identify a choice they would like to explore, without trying to make all the choices at once.

I have a similar experience with writing: often I am in a scene and I think of multiple choices a character could make and I can't focus on a single one, so I become paralysed and then distracted because it's too overwhelming. I am rarely distracted by one thing, I am often distracted by multiple possibilities at once.

I started to experiment with how I could usefully process all of these options. I said to myself that at the end of every session I would use my break to do the distractions, but that was making all my breaks too long and it was rare that tasks actually needed to be done straight away. A lot of them could be done a few days later, if they weren't about the current thing I was working on.

I also realised that if I had to hold all of these things in my head for later, it didn't actually stop them being a distraction. I needed to get them outside of my head, and put them in another container so I could not think about them, but trust I would re-engage with them later. This is where I began to play with a 'dump list'.

It's not a new idea, but again, I find it useful to give things names because then I can use the technique intentionally. A dump list is a place you can quickly dump the thoughts in your brain for later; it's a list of actions that need to be taken that are held temporarily in the list. Here are some general principles for a dump list:

1. It should be something that doesn't require effort to input. I use software called Asana to manage my tasks, but it takes a while to load it and add a task and categorise it. Instead, my dump list is a note on the home page of my phone – I add something in seconds and then forget about it.

2. It should be something you won't lose. I tend to find low-value items like notebooks are easier to lose than a phone, and also my phone is connected to a GPS tracker in case I lose it.

3. It should be on something you nearly always have on you. You don't just get random thoughts when you sit down to be

creative, you get them at all points of the day and if you end up with multiple dump lists you might lose something.

4. Set a rhythm for checking the list. I check it once a day, because I know it's rare that something needs to be done the same day. At the end of the day I either do some of the tasks if they can be done in under a minute, e.g. clean the cat litter, or add them to task management, e.g. cut the first four lines from that scene I wrote four days ago.

5. The important part is there being a system. If you know that anything that goes on there will be checked once each day, and then added to another long-term system like task management – then you don't actually have to remember to do any of that. There are rules that will remind you.

This means mine is a checkbox note pinned to the home page of my phone. I can get it out of my pocket in a few seconds, I don't need Wi-Fi to add anything to it, and I rarely leave my phone behind. An alarm goes off on my phone at the same time every day to check my dump list and see if anything needs doing.

I think some people have dump lists inside their own head; they have a thought and save the action for later and don't get distracted by it. I rarely find this is the case for ADHDers so I do it artificially instead.

You might find another solution, some people like notebooks, and there are many other apps that could be used. I have seen some artists have a separate email, and they email their distraction actions to themselves to check later. I know an actor who draws a box on the front of their scripts, and writes their dump list in there so it is always close to them.

TL;DR: Dump your thoughts in a list, and then set a regular point where you check them and action them.

1.2.8. Writing down things because you forget

You know that really good creative idea you had about four days ago, that you thought you'd remember, but when you came to actually apply it, you couldn't quite remember it? It's annoying isn't it?

If I learned anything from starting to use a dump list, it was that if something is not written down or documented immediately, then I was going to forget it.

There are some ideas I had during my research period that were lost because I couldn't retrieve them later. They might have become sections of this book but they floated away from my head and I couldn't remember them.

There are at least two reasons this is common for people with ADHD. The first is that it is well documented that ADHD often comes with some inefficiencies in working memory. Yes, I can remember things that happened years ago, but if someone tells me their phone number I will forget it before I have managed to get my phone out to write it down. Working memory is the short-term recall you often need when you're working.

The second reason is entirely unproven and more of a theory. I think that when I have creative ideas, I understand them similar to the way I understand distracting thoughts. They are very stimulating, not necessarily about the task at hand and often fleeting. I grew up being taught the value of focus, and so despite doing a lot of work on shame, there is still a deep-seated impulse to shut down distracting thoughts. Often this involves trying not to think about them, or devaluing them, as if I don't want to remember them. I think this is often what happens with creative ideas: I understand them like a distraction, and don't impulsively lean into them when I have them.

Both of these things mean I have to consciously distil the creative idea before it is lost. I thought the answer was to write them down immediately as I had them, but that brings up the usual challenges of thinking faster than I can write and losing notebooks.

Then a composer told me about how she records ideas on her phone and this was what I needed.

We need a way to capture ideas and often memos can be quicker. They can also more easily contain the feeling of the idea in the moment too, which is an important part of my creative process. They don't need to be totally comprehensive and make sense; they just need to contain enough information to be able to bring it out of your brain later.

I began using the voice-memo app on my phone to try and develop a practice of intentionally capturing creative ideas I had, before they were lost. It was difficult at first, I was quite self-conscious that it looked like I was walking down the street talking to myself. But it is like a muscle: the more you do it, the more you automatically document things before they are lost.

My voice-memo app can also transcribe the memos, which makes it easier to search through them when I need to find them later on. This has become something I rely on quite a lot now. I record most ideas that come to me, as soon as they come to me.

Whatever your recording mechanism is, it should be something where you can input information at the same speed as your thoughts and on a device that you often keep close to you. I know we always say we'll remember an idea and we don't need to bother documenting it, but we won't.

TL;DR: Create a rule that any idea must be captured, maybe in audio format, before you have another thought.

1.2.9. The doodle space

As part of my research, I went to a talk for people with ADHD about coping strategies. I won't name where it was but it did require a room full of people to sit quietly and listen to one person present some minimalist PowerPoint slides at the front. I am not convinced any of us paid attention to more than 20% of that talk.

Sometimes when I am researching a creative project or looking for inspiration, I need to listen to or watch something quite long. This is just how information is often distributed in the world. I know this is needed, but depending on where my brain is at, it is quite boring. I have a similar feeling in meetings if my collaborators and I are planning a creative project.

I think the instinct here is to take a fidget toy, so I have something to give me some extra stimulus while I listen. But I have probably bought fifty-plus fidget toys in the last few years, and I couldn't tell you where a single one of them is. The fewer 'things' I have, the fewer 'things' I can lose.

I am also quite bad at taking notes that are in any way readable, but I noticed I always have an instinct to start taking notes when I have to listen or pay attention to something for a long time. I rarely go back and look at the notes, I usually forget they exist, but there is something about the act of taking them that is useful.

What I found was that the act of writing was just enough to make a conversation stimulating enough so I could pay attention. It didn't really matter what I was writing – what mattered was that I was doing a second task at the same time to make sure my brain had enough to focus on. It stopped me being understimulated.

I started drawing a line down the right hand side of any notes I took to create a second margin, the point of that was to doodle anything I wanted. Sometimes I write keywords I hear, sometimes I draw what people are saying. I do anything that connects back to the thing I am listening to. Whatever it is, part of my page is for any notes I feel I should take, and the other part is for messy scribbles that will probably never be looked at again.

I also experimented with different kinds of paper: squared paper was an early win, because I could spend time colouring the squares in patterns while I listened. But I found that was a bit too distracting. Then I found dot-note paper, which is the one with little non-aligned dots on it. It gives me enough structure to make notes, draw lines, and doodle without trying to complete a pattern.

You don't need a separate notebook, you can just draw a line on whatever you normally use – e.g. a script – and give yourself permission to have a messy, pointless space to help you focus.

I am tempted to say that it is also quite discreet, that people notice a fidget toy, but taking notes is something that blends in. But I don't want to suggest that our aim has to be to appear neurotypical all the time. It often can be helpful to blend in more, because then we don't have to expend energy on answering questions when we don't want to. But it should also not be our default position. I use doodle spaces because it's too easy to lose fidget toys. The fact that nobody asks me questions is a by-product of that choice.

TL;DR: Give yourself an area in notes to doodle impulsively while listening to something, to make the lecture/conversation a bit more stimulating.

1.2.10. Days off, emotional dysregulation and unmasking

I am not known as an angry person. I'm actually known as being quite calm, and part of this is that I have really effectively trained myself to manage that particular emotion in order to resist being labelled with the common 'angry young boy' stereotype that a lot of kids were labelled with where I grew up. This is often called 'masking', the act of performing a version of yourself that is more acceptable to society.

There are benefits to this: it allows me to navigate spaces I otherwise would be barred from because I don't meet the social codes. But it is also a silencing of something that I naturally experience.

This doesn't mean that I don't experience anger; my emotions are generally quite unpredictable and tend to consume a lot of my energy when they are pushed beyond normality. A lot of the ADHDers I spoke to while doing research had a similar experience, especially those that had grown to understand their ADHD as an adult. We had a lack of emotional regulation so we experienced a lot of big feelings, but we had developed some kind of coping mechanism for managing that.

It takes effort though, and requires a level of performance that is quite emotionally draining a lot of the time. I find that if I have to contain things too often, then I struggle to write as much because I'm not really connecting with my emotions.

Sometimes, when I can't write, I look at what I've been doing recently and I see that I've been doing a lot of masking. It's not just with emotional dysregulation this happens; I mask for lots of reasons, but this is the thing that most affects me getting creative work done.

In order to focus, I need to have a regular outlet to unmask. I need dedicated time where I'm not doing the draining work of appearing more 'normal'. Sometimes writing is that – sometimes I see huge emotions emerge in shows I am working on because I need it to go somewhere.

But as I've grappled more with being an ADHDer, I've tried to structure in time when I can intentionally unmask without it entering my creativity.

This ultimately comes down to making sure I properly plan days off. These days off don't have to be relaxing in the typical sense – I don't need to go to a spa or have a fancy brunch – I just need times when I have the space to commit to what my natural impulses are. These days normally include very unstructured time. I don't want to choose when to do things, I just want to follow my impulses with no expectations. Sometimes those impulses are to do nothing.

Unmasking isn't just emotion. I love having days where I just don't do the washing-up if my brain isn't allowing me to do that. I love having days where I can just do whatever I am hyperfocusing on at that time, and stop as soon as I get bored and do something else. Yes, I have to deal with the consequences of not washing up at some point, but I can plan for that too.

Often my most productive creative days follow days like this. Writing within my mask stops me being authentic with myself, and it is so deeply ingrained that I need to do some real work to take it off over a day.

Later in this book I'll go into more detail about masking, or you can flip to that section now if you want a more in-depth exploration of it.

TL;DR: Plan appropriate time off, so you can stop masking your ADHD, and be authentic with yourself when being creative.

1.2.11. Relaxed performances and processes

As I gathered all of these techniques, I found myself describing the way I make work as 'relaxed'. I didn't mean I did it from a sun lounger, I had drawn the language from relaxed performances in theatre.

Relaxed performances in theatre are not new any more; they happen increasingly often. In a relaxed performance the sensory environment of a theatre is changed to make it more accessible, which might include everything from changing the lighting in a show to turning off the hand-dryers in the toilets as they are quite loud.

This creates an atmosphere where people are able to make voluntary noises, because there is no expectation of silence. Relaxed performances are most often considered to be aimed at autistic people, but they are really helpful for a huge array of people. You can pretty much rely on the fact that a relaxed performance will tell you if there are strobe lights, which is handy for people that have any kind of photo-sensitive epilepsy. I quite like relaxed performances because I fidget a lot while watching theatre. I am not a fan of sitting still in a cramped seat for hours on end. If my attention slows for a while, this is not a comment on the theatre I'm watching; I just do something like scroll on my phone to manage my stimulus.

Now there are companies that make performances relaxed as standard. In this model we are not making work and then removing things from it, but we are making theatre where the full articulation of the art can be experienced by more people.

We are also relaxing the process of making theatre. We can relax a rehearsal process, which is often called an 'accessible' rehearsal process. The problem with that is that 'accessible' is a broad term: accessible for whom? It can't be accessible for everyone, as people have different and clashing needs a lot of the time.

To say a process of making something is 'relaxed' is to say that the social codes that are normally upheld are actively disrupted, to allow for more relaxed behaviours. You might relax a rehearsal process by explicitly stating any expectations can be broken, by including an access worker in the room who can support people, or by planning the rehearsal process to happen more slowly to accommodate people's needs.

As I felt myself drawn towards the language of 'relaxing', I also began to ask people how we might relax other processes, spaces and tasks you have to do for work.

Here are some ways that things might become relaxed, with specific attention to people with ADHD.

Meetings	<ul><li>You can fidget.</li><li>Eye contact is not required to confirm someone is listening.</li><li>If the meeting is online, you can leave your camera off if that works better for you.</li><li>Someone is nominated to take notes so other people can participate without multitasking.</li></ul>
Rehearsals	<ul><li>Have a breakout space with low stimulus (lower lights and sounds and soft things) that people can use if they want to.</li><li>It's fine to be late – in fact, this is factored into the schedule.</li><li>More breaks in rehearsal days to accommodate energy levels. In these breaks there are still some activities people can do if they want to, if they are in a productive phase of their day.</li><li>People can leave the space when they want to.</li></ul>
Auditions	<ul><li>There are no surprise requests.</li><li>Pictures of the panel with names are sent in advance.</li><li>Like a job interview, the things the panel wants to see are sent in advance.</li><li>There is an explicit communication of when the audition starts and stops; no cutting people off halfway through.</li></ul>

Networking/ industry events	• No requirement to participate in any specific social codes or activities (people can take time out). • Nobody needs to pretend they have to go somewhere if they want to leave. There should be explicit permission/instruction that people should leave when they feel ready.

These are not exhaustive lists, but they might be useful to help you begin to explore how to relax other areas of creative work. The concept of 'relaxing' a process is just the act of identifying which expectations are barriers, and relaxing them so they do not exist any more. It reduces the need for masking and management techniques, and means people can work to the best of their ability.

If you want to think more about the act of relaxing performances or processes, then I would recommend keeping an eye on the work of an organisation called Touretteshero.

TL;DR: Relaxed performances are great, and you can relax anything by applying the same principles.

1.2.12. Finish on a high

Throughout all of these techniques, I've explored a toolkit for how to be more productive when being creative. But there is also another important aspect which I touched upon in the previous sections.

When you're done with your practice for the day, it's important to switch off in some way in order not to burn out before the next session. This is easier said than done.

I often finish a writing day feeling quite hyperfocused on what still needs to be done, and my head is whirring about characters and choices I could make. This can be helpful, but it can also be debilitating to getting some proper rest, and when I don't rest most of my ADHD traits get worse.

The worst days are when I finish on a task that is only half completed. I cannot break the focus I've worked hard to create and relax; I am constantly thinking about what needs to be done. It can become a bit like an addiction, and it makes it difficult to sleep.

It is a not dissimilar feeling to starting a day where I am struggling to get my brain in to gear, and by the end of the day I struggle to get it out. This similarity led me to wondering if there was a technique for switching off at the end of a day. In the same way I suggested leaving a gift for the first session of the day, could I leave myself one for the end of the day too?

I didn't want to create a desire to keep going, I wanted to create a sense of an ending. It's like telling yourself a story, I wanted a sense of conclusion so I could get out of the work day.

I began trying to leave myself a gift for the end of the day, something that was easily completable, and that would create some satisfaction. If you have a group of subtasks, find one that logically feels like an ending and let that be the last one of the day. The easiest one, if all else fails, is to print the section of script I have been working on, to create a thing I can hold in my hand.

When I spoke to actors, they told me this was a bit like how they found cool-downs useful at the end of a rehearsal. We focus so much on warm-ups in theatre rehearsals, and less on cool-downs because people normally have to dash to get home. But a cool-down does create a sense of detachment.

Finishing on a completed task lets my brain break the focus on working, and move on to whatever thing I'm going to become interested by in the evening.

This is easier said than done, and isn't always possible, depending on your practice, but it became increasingly important for me to try and find one every day.

TL;DR: Always finish a day of sessions on a completed task.

1.2.13. The ADHD form

As I looked back on the techniques I had found, I began to wonder how this would change the work I would make in future: would I suddenly find a form of ADHD theatre? In a moment of wondering, I nicknamed it the 'Theatre of Distraction' and that drew my attention to another writer I had often thought of as very distracted. I allowed myself some time to think about this, and see where it led, something I had been resisting so far because I was so focused on cracking the secret to productivity.

There was a playwright called Bertolt Brecht – he's been dead a long time, but that guy cannot tell a story in a straight line. I've always enjoyed his work and the things he wrote about the creative process, and re-reading his work in the context of doing my research gave me some clues as to why.

The dominant theory of how to write theatre in the UK is that characters make sense and we follow each characters' journey over the course of three acts. A protagonist pursues something, encounters barriers along the way, and may or may not achieve what they pursue.

This produces a lot of realism in the UK, a lot of plays that claim to be about real life. But my real life is not as linear or neat as this. I generally get distracted or overwhelmed before I reach a lot of goals, unless I exert a lot of effort (as described in this book) to make sure I get there.

Brecht doesn't do this as much, his characters often have a related core but not a related logic from one scene to the next. Generally the narrative gets distracted and goes on huge tangents before you get to where you are supposed to be. Most of his characters are prone to bursts of oversharing and high emotion, as if they are experiencing some emotional dysregulation. He is not generally interested in audiences being absorbed and believing everything they see, but intentionally draws our attention to bigger ideas we're supposed to think about while watching the play.

Brecht's work offers me a closer representation of how my brain works than most other famous writers. I don't know if I believe in diagnosing people with ADHD after they have died, but I do think there are huge similarities about how a lot of ADHD brains work and how Brecht's brain worked.

Rejection sensitivity (and a lot of imposter syndrome) had made me try to create work that could be accepted in the value system of what is a 'good' play. But this idea of good has been formed by a lot of neurotypical writers and creatives who had a different experience of self, and psychology, and emotion to me. Yes, my characters might be prone to sudden outbursts of emotion which some people find too on the nose, but I am also prone to sudden outbursts of emotion so that is very realistic for me.

I began to give myself permission to create bad writing, to explore where my work would go if I committed to my impulses, and distractions, and lack of ability to prioritise. This point might seem to go against everything I have said so far in the book, but I think it's important to recognise that there are things we have to do in order to get projects done and get paid, and there is this lovely world where we just wander through distractions and do creative things.

If we commit to that lovely world, then often the form our creativity takes will change.

I've used writing as an example, but as I had conversations with other creatives about this, they also had their suspicions about whether the forms they were working in were really as unchangeable as they were led to believe. The common factor stopping them was that they thought that would make bad art or creativity.

I worked with an actor who was quite new to an ADHD diagnosis a few years ago, and he commented that he found it easier to find his way through the emotional journey of my characters than he had with other roles. We talked about how his experience of drama school had been focused on learning to centre himself, to stop fidgeting, and to become a person who seemed more neurotypical. For once, he wasn't having to 'perform' as much as he was having to 'live' the role. Some roles often require actors to perform neurotypicality as well as performing the role, but this additional work goes unspoken and unsupported.

I'm not suggesting that all people with ADHD must reject forms created by neurotypical people, or that all ADHD writers must like Brecht. But I do think it's important to remember that our creativity might look different to someone else's, and the sectors we work in might not value that right away.

'Good' art is usually defined by neurotypical people, and trying to fit into that box is not the only option for us. If the thing you can create is radically different to what people would consider 'good' because your brain works differently, maybe we shouldn't constantly try to manage that away.

The problem here is that those of us who use creativity to pay our rent will find it a little challenging to commit to bucking the trend of our value system. This is where neurodivergent people often pick up their shame. We can be perfectly comfortable and happy with our process at first, but we are often encouraged to manage it away so that we can produce work that is more sellable.

I don't want to manage my natural impulses; I feel very at ease with them now, but I often find I need to do it in order to make a living. The trick is to do the techniques in this book while still dreaming up how it might be different. That's why I wrote the later parts of this book: I had to simultaneously find a way to live in the world, while also trying to change how it works.

TL;DR: ADHD might change the art you create, not just the process of making the art. Sometimes, we should let ourselves explore that, instead of using techniques to manage it.

1.2.14. Don't write

As I grappled with the techniques I had been finding, they weren't giving me immediate solutions. There were days when I just couldn't get the writing out, and there still are.

There was one time when I had put aside an entire day to write, I had cleared my schedule around other work and I had planned to get a lot of writing done, so I went to a coffee shop. No sooner had I sat at my laptop than it was 1 p.m. and I had hardly written anything, then I had lunch and suddenly I found it was 4 p.m. That time is closer to the end of the day than the start and I went around in circles trying to force myself to write with techniques until I sat and cried. Crying into an iced Americano felt a bit ridiculous as an adult, but I was so disappointed in myself at the time. I had put in so much effort to create what I thought were the perfect conditions, and I couldn't do something simple that I was claiming to be good at.

I didn't sleep well for days, which is my normal reaction when I am frustrated about something. I went in search of some sleep solutions, and found a great article. It said that if you can't sleep, don't lie in bed: go and do something else. When struggling to sleep, it is easy to develop an association between the frustration you feel, and the act of sleeping, until you feel frustrated as soon as you get into bed.

The same goes for ADHD and your creative practice. I think, if you are trying to write/learn lines/paint and you're getting frustratingly distracted, the only thing left to do is stop trying to do the thing. Our brains are complicated, and sometimes there is no technique that will help.

Sometimes the only thing you can do is stop and do something else, to preserve your relationship with your practice. It felt like a defeat to admit that, but if I'm honest with myself then it's important.

The exception here comes if there is a hard deadline, or if you're in an environment where you're being paid to bring your creativity at a specific time, like an actor. There are at least two possible ways to alleviate this, depending on your process:

I can add baggage time into my writing schedule, so that deadlines are always set about a day before they get really urgent. But this is not possible for some people.

I never commit to only one big project, or at least I try not to. I am always working on multiple plays, and if I can't find the focus for one, sometimes I find I get distracted into writing another one.

It takes a lot of planning and a lot of bravery to not do your practice. A lot of people who do creative things are made to feel lucky that they get to do this. It's true, the world should be built in such a way that people can be creative when they want, but it's not – and you can't shoulder all the responsibility for that. Sometimes it's okay to not do your thing. You are not being ungrateful, sometimes you need to give yourself permission to do that in order to have the headspace to do it better later.

TL;DR: Sometimes your brain just won't cooperate, so plan some buffer time to allow yourself to take time off on these days.

Questions to ask yourself:	Doodle space
• How could body doubling help here? • Could you need more micro-deadlines? • How could you game-ify this? • Do you need a break? • How could your sensory input be better? • Do you feel like you're masking?	
Your dump list (distractions for later):	
What is your finishing gift?	

1.3. I can't get it finished

1.3.1. *It's always longer than you think*

As I got to the end of my research project, I decided I would apply those techniques in writing a new script. I set up the entire project, planned it out, and as I got towards the end of that script, I somehow still ran out of time and had to rush at the end.

At no point did I significantly get behind schedule, or get particularly frustrated or distracted, I just do not know how long it takes to do things.

ADHD often involves a certain amount of time-blindness, which means you don't really notice the passing of time. This is how you end up daydreaming or hyperfocusing and suddenly a lot of time has passed.

It also means I don't have a good natural grasp of how long tasks take me – they can vary so wildly – and I am often not really paying attention properly to the time passing while I do them.

This means that I had massively underestimated the time it would take me to finish the last parts of the script, the thing I struggle with the most.

I need to overplan the amount of time I need to finish something. It needs a sense of urgency and a deadline, but it needs one that I know I can achieve without having to default to a disappointing all-nighter, despite having stayed on track with the project thus far.

This section is incredibly short. The first rule of finishing a project is that it will always take longer than you think. Write it on the wall, tattoo it on your forehead, do whatever it takes to remember it.

TL;DR: Overplan the amount of time you need to do the last stage of a project.

1.3.2. The last 10% takes 30% of the effort

Much like this bit of the chapter, there is always that last 10% of the task that needs doing and it is nearly always the hardest.

I quite like working out how to do something, it's really stimulating. I love working out where a character might go and how they might change. Once I've worked it out though, actually making that happen is difficult. It's a common experience, when you get to the last 10% of lines to learn/canvas to paint/song to write – you can see the light at the end of the tunnel and suddenly it's very unstimulating.

Once you can see the final thing fully formed, it feels like you have done the work, and completing the project suddenly feels less exciting.

For me as a writer, that last 10% is always proofreading. I can spell really well, but you would not believe that if you read early drafts of my writing. The concept of going through something I've expended all this energy on as soon as I've written it, looking for detailed typos is absolutely not something my brain has any interest in. It may have said I had a good attention to detail on my day-job CVs for years, but it was never true.

Depending on your practice, there are lots of things that can help with the final 10%. I use a lot of grammar and punctuation software to help with proofreading, because otherwise I would never do it. If anyone offers to proofread something, I will bite their hand off.

For other practices this is not so simple, and the only way I have found to do the last 10% is to game-ify it to the point of abstraction, and overplan it.

For example, if I really need to proofread a script, I will normally do it backwards, because it breaks the monotony of re-reading something I have already written in the order I wrote it. I will also create a subtask list of each page and cross them off my list as I go.

When you plan your time, don't imagine that your progress towards a target happens in a linear fashion. For me, the first 10% is very quick, the next 40% is very slow, the beginning of the second half tends to speed up slightly, and then the final 10% takes the longest.

I aim to spend 30% of my energy to finish the final 10% of a project. This often means setting myself a false deadline earlier than the actual deadline, and creating an external accountability structure.

TL;DR: The final 10% of something should be game-ified, subtasked and you should allow for 30% of the time to complete that 10%.

1.3.3. Have something in the drawer

I am writing this last section looking at a pile of knitting in my living room, a half-finished bear which was one of my lockdown hobbies that never got finished. My creative projects can sometimes be like that too; unfinished because as soon as I see the end, my brain starts to think about the next thing.

There is no magical solution to this. I don't want to deny my creative attention so that I lose the momentum on another project, but I do need to finish the one I am currently working on.

I was taught by two friends called Jen and Rob a long time ago, never to be only working on one project. It is always helpful to have different projects at different stages. If you are relying on the success of just one thing you're working on, and it doesn't get to where it is supposed to, it's crushing and there is nothing else.

If something doesn't go well, and you can whip out of your drawer another script that needs a redraft, it offers you a way forward.

This has always been really helpful with ADHD as well. It comes back to my focus on making projects iterative. If I get something to a first draft and then rotate to redrafting something else, it gives me a variety that I enjoy.

Swapping to another project makes the first one feel new again as well, and then the difficult ending part will feel a little bit exciting again.

If I have three big projects I need to finish in a year, then I could complete one, and then the other, and then the third, but that's going to be difficult for me. If I break each one up into stages or drafts, then rotating between them means the difficult last 10% is always a bit smaller. The final push isn't such a mountain, but a regular hill I need to climb every month, which is much better for my stamina.

I think of this as having something waiting in the drawer I could work on at all times, so I can take that productive detour.

TL;DR: Plan projects in rotation, so that you are never reliant on only one.

1.3.4. Do you need to finish?

This might be cheating. It might be that I know I need to finish this book and I'm pretending that I might not need to.

As I got towards the end of this research period, I looked back at all the knowledge I had gained, and next to the notes was a play. It was something I had tried to write a while ago and it was technically unfinished; I knew how it should end but I hadn't written the last bit yet.

I had a sudden thought of a different ending and over the next day or so, I wrote that ending. It wasn't as neat, but it was more interesting than what I had originally intended. If I had finished that play when I had originally written it, it would have been much more boring.

This made me ask myself: does everything have to be finished?

Sometimes the answer is yes. Sometimes you must get to the end or you won't have finished the project or possibly get paid for it.

Sometimes the answer might be no. Sometimes it might be helpful for something to be intentionally unfinished.

What happens if we fail to complete a task?

People like Jack Halberstam have written extensively (usually essays but there are good blogs and YouTube videos too) about failure, and about how if we were successful all the time then nothing really would change. To be successful all the time is to assimilate into the dominant structure of the world, to become the thing that is making your life difficult. To be successful in this case, might be to perform being neurotypical.

Failure, on the other hand, can lead to unexpected change. Failing to finish that script fully, and then committing to that failure, gave me the freedom to experiment with different endings. I wouldn't have learned that if I had resolved everything neatly.

This is not a practical suggestion and it is not always workable. But I do believe there is some courage in accepting how your brain works, and allowing that to influence what creativity exists in the world.

It is this thought that made me realise my research wasn't over. Yes, I had a list of techniques that would help me be productive, but they were basically helping me appear neurotypical. I wasn't so sure I did want that all the time, and I held this thought as I worked out what to do next.

TL;DR: Sometimes it's okay not to finish something. Sometimes we can learn from that.

THE LAST 10% WILL TAKE LONGER THAN YOU THINK.

Now we have a list of techniques, all our problems are solved, right? Not quite.

As I marched forward with my research notes to advocate for myself in the industry, I overheard someone in the office of my day job complaining about the number of people in the arts suddenly claiming they had ADHD.

This is not an uncommon comment, which I've heard a few times since, as if people that are drawn to creative professions have some strange desire to go through the relatively gruelling diagnostic process for ADHD.

I mainly work in the theatre sector and it is a relatively welcoming and aware bit of the world. Organisations funded by Arts Council England have to consider inclusivity in their plans, and it is becoming more common that people's access needs are taken into account in the workplace. But I still do find that sometimes there's a difference between what people do, and what people believe.

It's not often, but in some rooms there are comments from people with influence that boil down to them not believing that people have ADHD.

They can see the need for step-free access, they can see the need for BSL knowledge, they can see that some people communicate in obviously different ways. They cannot see what is happening inside my brain, and considering I went undiagnosed for twenty years, I have become very good at hiding it.

When my colleague made this comment, I told them a story which I had picked up from some reading in my research project. This is not originally my story, but it's a version of some incredible research done by Thom Hartmann, and I hope I can tell it effectively.

Imagine a long time ago there was a person called Charlie. I am talking a very long time ago, when Charlie mainly had to hunt in order to find food. The fact that Charlie got distracted easily made it very difficult for creatures to sneak up on them. They felt very comfortable sleeping for short bursts, and then travelling, and then sleeping again. The ability to become intensely focused on a hunt for a short amount of time would have been useful for the final stages of catching prey. It could be argued that Charlie's brain was incredibly similar to what we now might think is the brain of an ADHDer.

But then, Charlie's friend Alex decided to put a lot of useful plants in one specific area and farming was born. Charlie found this boring, to do the same thing every day, but Alex really excelled at the repetition. As generations progressed, Alex's family also begun keeping animals in specific areas so they didn't have to hunt any more. This idea caught on, and suddenly a lot of people were farming, on a regular daily, monthly and annual cycle. Slowly this became the preferred method to survive, and the people who were good at it would live longer.

Cut forward thousands of years, all the way to the Industrial Revolution. Although people weren't hunting, Charlie's descendants had at least learned that there was some use for their brains in crafting. They made incredible shoes from scratch, each one different according to the needs of the user. However, one of Alex's descendants had the great idea of opening a shoe factory, and its mass production slowly put independent shoemakers out of business. Instead of making an entire shoe, Charlie's family would sit on a conveyor belt making the same type of shoelace all day every day. This repetition, lack of variety, and need to focus for a long time made it difficult to be a good employee.

In order to control these factories, the owners decided there was a working day: people would arrive at a certain time and leave at a certain time, so the owners could control how much to pay the workers. This felt logical, but suddenly people needed to focus for a long amount of time with few breaks, and then squeeze all their rest into one overnight window instead of having any variety. One bad night's sleep, and focus would drop, and the next work day would be even worse.

Cut even further forward into the future, to the invention of office life. Unsurprisingly, Alex's family excel at sitting in grey boxes, doing similar tasks on repeat all day with very little meaning. They enjoy pushing emails between people, working exactly the same hours every day, and waiting for the weekend when they can intentionally switch off. In fact, these jobs become much better paid than anything else, and it becomes easier to access food because they can go to Waitrose.

In contrast, Charlie's descendants find themselves incompatible with this labour and after struggling for five years with office jobs, they become creative freelancers. They make much less money, and have much worse access to food and stability, but at least they occasionally get something done.

The tables have turned. The type of brain that once upon a time had an enhanced chance of getting food and safety, now has a much worse chance. The type of brain that made a bad hunter can suddenly work in more corporate office environments and enjoy modern inventions, like Deliveroo and pensions.

When I tell versions of this story to people, I am amazed when they wonder why people with ADHD are often attracted to a varied, 'choose your own hours' job focused on what they are passionate about.

The history of ADHD might not be the history of a disorder – it might be the history of a type of brain that has become increasingly incompatible with how we expect people to do labour and access food and safety. I prefer to think of it the other way around: that the world is becoming incompatible with my brain, because it is the world that is changing, not necessarily my brain.

This relies on some research which is ongoing, but as a story it does offer some context and understanding to something which we understand very little about.

It offered me a lot of context and permission to begin advocating for myself in the sector in a way that wasn't focused on my medical needs, but how I need the world to work. It is the world which is becoming increasingly incompatible with me, and that is a choice – we have chosen to change how labour works. If there has ever been a choice, there is always the option to choose something different.

This is what I wanted to start exploring: what if I didn't just look for techniques that help me exist in this world, what would it look like if the world changed? Or at least to start with, what would it be like if the sector I work in changed?

I knew I needed to make a show and put it out into the world, but I also knew that I was reimagining my whole self at the same time, and so I would need some help. Artist-development programmes in the theatre sector are abundant, but they are rarely in-depth. They often revolve around free workshops, and some self-guided time for exploration.

Luckily, I managed to get a place on a programme called Starting Blocks, which is run by Camden People's Theatre. It's a guided attachment, with funding included (at least in the year I did it), where you are brought into a peer cohort to explore making a new show. This is exactly what I needed, it had all the elements I had found in Part One: body doubling with the peer group, managing micro-deadlines with regular check-ins, and it was focused on making work in a room rather than behind a desk.

I set out to make a show called *Education, Education, Karaoke*, about state education in the UK and the divides it often creates in working-class communities. Part Two contains the stories of how I learned to navigate the sector while applying all the research I had done already.

2.1. Telling people you have ADHD

2.1.1. Why is telling people difficult?

As I have tried to articulate in the story above, our brains are often operating in a world that has been built to be increasingly incompatible with us.

This is not how a lot of the world understands ADHD. If you're diagnosed when young, people often don't try to change the world around you – they try to give you techniques so you stop being a problem. If you're diagnosed as an adult then there is often a belief that follows you saying that you made it to adulthood, so you don't need help.

The first time I tried to ask for help with something because of my understanding of my ADHD, I felt such intense shame and like I was a fraud. I had gone to university, had some success in my jobs and moved to a city over two hundred miles away from where I grew up. It appeared I was 'adulting' really well, and if I had made it this far, surely I should be able to keep going.

The thing is, that history is littered with invisible things. At the end of my three years at university I got so overwhelmed and had a meltdown so big that I made myself incredibly ill and my parents had to drive and get me. When I first moved to London I did not have any control over impulse spending so I got into debt. Yes, I had hustled to be successful in jobs but I had generally not stayed in any one of them for longer than nine months, until I got bored and moved on to a different one.

These are the stories we are encouraged not to tell, and I think shame often sits in the gap between the version of us that people know, and the version of us that we know. I have often felt shame about these truths about myself; I feel like my inner life should match up with how my life appears on the outside. The more shame I feel about my inner life, the bigger I make the gap between the two versions of me. It has become a sort of mission of mine to close that gap.

It's also the difference in this void that my fraudulent feelings lie. The version of me that a lot of people see is not the version of me that I experience. If there wasn't shame, if I had more effectively told the stories I am telling now, they might know the real version of me and asking for help would have been easier.

I'll talk more about these feelings of shame and what to do with them in the third part of this book, but here I want to recognise that they exist for a lot of people.

Asking for help is often incredibly difficult.

At first I tried to think of it as advocating for my needs, but this still felt like it was singling out some kind of deficiency I had.

I eventually found the language of 'access' was where I felt more comfortable. When you recognise and accept that the world is not built for you, that there are walls everywhere, you can then ask for access. Instead of struggling to climb over the wall, there are people in the world who can easily make doors appear, so we can go right through or, even better, take the wall down.

We don't hesitate to ask someone to hold the door open when our hands are full – in that moment our immediate world is not built for us, and we are asking for someone to remove the barrier in front of us.

Asking for help, or advocating for yourself, or telling someone about your access requirements is a difficult thing to do. But identifying a way you can understand it is important. Look for times in your life where you find it easier to ask for help, and think about what language could help recreate those scenarios.

Reducing the gap between yourself, and the external perception of you, goes hand in hand with giving yourself more permission to ask for help.

TL;DR: You are allowed to ask for help. Remember this if you don't remember anything else in this book.

2.1.2. When to talk about ADHD

When I knew I was going to be applying to the Starting Blocks programme, I had to decide whether I was going to be honest and tell them I was looking to relearn a practice that had become increasingly unhelpful to me, or tell a lie.

The reason it felt difficult was because I had worked with the theatre before, and never said anything about it, because I didn't know. I was anxious that they might react how my colleague reacted at the beginning of this part, and question the truth of what I had to say.

I considered applying and keeping it private, but I knew I would not be able to do my best work if I wasn't honest with them eventually.

The thought of telling them after starting the programme seemed worse. By that point the gap between what they understood about me, and what I understood about myself would be bigger. The shame would be stronger.

I decided to be honest upfront, so they knew I was exploring my practice in light of a new understanding about my ADHD. This was the first time I had applied for something and told them, and actually everything was fine and nobody really found it difficult to understand.

The imagined scenario was much worse than the reality.

This is a specific case and sometimes imagined realities do still come true. I know of actors that have disclosed access needs at the audition stage and have been automatically discounted because that feels too complicated for the casting director.

The entire first part of this book is a toolkit of techniques to help you do your creative practice – in order to do these, you often need small adjustments or understandings from people around you. In order to do your best work, it is in your interest to be honest sooner rather than later.

Often the arts and culture sectors can feel incredibly small, and like we have to say yes to everything that comes our way. Sometimes this is true; I don't want to pretend there is a utopia because money is still real. If you are making your best work, then the smallness of the sector works in your favour, as suddenly the friends of that collaborator/commissioner/employer hear about how great your work is too.

Whenever we tell someone about our ADHD we are helping to de-stigmatise it. The more people hear it, the more it feels common and normal to have these conversations.

TL;DR: Telling people early will help you advocate for yourself sooner.

2.1.3. How to talk about ADHD

When I first started talking about ADHD, I thought of my experience of growing up with epilepsy. It felt similar because it was in some way related to my brain, but my memories of epilepsy were in the context of receiving a lot of emergency medical care. I stopped breathing during my first seizure and for every seizure after, we would wait to find out whether that would happen again.

It seemed silly in comparison to talk about ADHD in the same way, it didn't have the same sense of medical urgency to it. ADHD in itself brings no immediate threat to life unless I forget my keys again in the middle of winter and get stuck outside my flat waiting for someone to let me in.

At first I alternated between two ideas:

1. I would play it down, I would make self-deprecating jokes and only feel able to bring it up if I minimised it.

2. I would play it up, I would include as many words as possible that made it feel more urgent. I would call it 'severe' or 'complex' ADHD, or use highly technical terms, and these were a defence and a justification for advocating for my needs.

Neither of these things really served me well. The first meant that people thought I would never need support – I would tell a joke and then the conversation about any adjustments never followed. The second was a defence, which largely made people nervous so they found it difficult to engage with conversations about my needs.

'Severe' and 'complex' are words that can be used in regards to ADHD, but I also think they can be a way of trying to protect ourselves. The by-product of this can be the creation of a culture where we're trying to portray ourselves as worse than the next neurodivergent person.

Advocating for your needs is important, but doing that in solidarity with other people is more important. If you get your needs met, but it requires someone else to play up their needs in future, that's quite a toxic cycle.

It is understandable. When I began reading more about ADHD, I was struck by the number of neurodivergent people who had gone into academia, or who talked about their experience in highly technical ways. Big words are a good defence against a world that does not want to meet your needs.

But also, it doesn't always help general understanding if the exclusive way we talk about ADHD is quite technical.

While I had the opportunity to try out telling people in a welcoming environment, I began to make a list of how I wanted talk about ADHD. These rules tried to balance the need to explain things comprehensively in order to get my needs met, without having to make the explanation overly technical.

These loose rules became the following list:

1. Firstly, I aim to be accurate, firm and conversational about telling people. No jokes, no exaggeration, little complexity.

2. Then if I need to elaborate on my needs more, I allow the complexity to exist in the needs, but not in my condition. For example, I would explain the complexities of body doubling, as opposed to explaining why I am not great at external accountability.

3. If I need to explain more, then I'll generally talk about having poor executive functioning. I'll elaborate on this later, but it's basically the set of skills that allows you to organise information.

These are the rules I settled on in order to advocate for myself as I began to make this show. There is no fixed way to talk about ADHD, but I still find it useful to resist more urgent language in most scenarios. Everyone will find their own balance of how they want to talk about it, but don't feel like you have to adopt one of the main ways people often talk about it.

TL;DR: You don't have to reach for jokes or complexity when telling people about ADHD.

2.1.4. Beginning to unmask

Once I got into the Starting Blocks programme, I began to experiment with unmasking. I hadn't realised I was masking for a long time, but once I discovered the term I began looking for the moments of slight discomfort and to notice the ways I was trying to manage my appearance.

I became aware of ADHD as an adult, and so I had subconsciously developed coping mechanisms to hide it during my childhood. My least favourite of these is that in order not to visibly fidget, I began picking my nails because it can be done invisibly under the table while you're supposed to be sat still in class. This is a really tangible example, but some things are more subtle.

For example, I had a specific face I pulled to demonstrate I was listening to someone. I realised I was listening for the right moment to nod or make a sound, instead of actually listening. I was performing the act of listening to reassure the other person. I normally listen best when I can look around and fidget and get that extra stimulation that helps me to listen. The act of performing listening even functioned as a distraction from the more natural way I pay attention to people. It took a lot of effort to give myself permission to not look at people while they were talking, and at first I felt like I had to let people know this was happening.

I have always had a bad habit of interrupting people, which comes from my impulsiveness. If I hear something that is really interesting to me, I can't resist starting to talk about it. In order to manage this, I had created a very shy and withdrawn persona I could hide in, and performing this character allowed me to observe the conversation as opposed to properly participating in it. This has been the hardest thing to unmask, and I am still learning to do it now. It created a persona which has come to define how people understand me, and as I tried to stop using it, I think people were confused as to where it had gone.

These three specific examples are the ones I worked out in the early stage of my development time at Camden People's Theatre, in the initial meetings. I was paying attention to when I was having to exert mental effort without intentionally doing it.

I think I only began to notice those things, because I had told people I was re-finding my practice after learning about my ADHD. I could be openly experimental in what I was doing. I didn't feel a pressure to mask, because people could contextualise what was happening better.

It is difficult to unmask without 'coming out' or telling people you have ADHD, because often we need people to have some context as to why we might behave in ways they are not used to. But once this happens, it does give you the freedom to experiment with unmasking.

TL;DR: Telling people you have ADHD lets you more actively watch for the ways you have learned to mask and undo them.

2.1.5. Access riders

When I started the programme, a friend suggested I make an access rider to lay out my needs. I didn't quite understand what one was at first, so a friend shared theirs with me.

An access rider is an advocacy document, which means you don't have to articulate your needs to a collaborator/employer/commissioner over and over again, because you've done it once and written it down.

The process of making an access rider is clearer for some people more than others; those people with very tangible access requirements can write things that people find easy to understand.

It can be more challenging with ADHD for two reasons. Firstly, the formation of an ADHD community is relatively new and therefore it is only more recently that we have begun to share tips and techniques to help each other understand what we might need. As the knowledge is in its infancy and not widely available, we often don't know what we can ask for.

Secondly, the barriers that people with ADHD face are often baked into the structures we exist in and made invisible. Some barriers are incredibly tangible: for example, steps which make buildings inaccessible to a variety of people. It's not easy to change those things, but we are better at imagining the solution. It is more challenging for people to imagine how they might remove the requirement of productivity from their practice, and people struggle to imagine how they might allow you to be late with deadlines without making you feel lazy. Often to meet the needs of someone with ADHD, it requires people around you to rethink how they understand things like time, urgency and social interaction.

These are very intangible things, so here follows a non-exhaustive list of possible additions to your access rider, and questions you might ask yourself in common categories. I am not suggesting you should need these, but they give examples of the ways you might think about your access needs.

TIME	<ul><li>Breaks at least once an hour.</li><li>Someone to set micro-deadlines with you.</li><li>Flexible deadlines.</li><li>At least one week's notice of a change of time for something.</li><li>Where and when is your time management worse? How can people make that less stressful for you?</li></ul>
SPACE	<ul><li>A breakout space where you can go and decompress.</li><li>Rooms where the temperature is comfortable, and can be changed.</li><li>What makes a space good for you?</li><li>What makes a space bad for you?</li></ul>
TRAVEL	<ul><li>Clear instructions, including a postcode if you need to get somewhere.</li><li>At least one week's notice if there is a location change.</li><li>If anything changes less than a week in advance, someone should call instead of leaving an email in case it is missed.</li><li>Do you want to be booked in the quiet carriage on a train?</li><li>Do you want to arrive somewhere at least an hour in advance, so you have time to decompress from travel before something happens?</li></ul>

	• Do you prefer to travel between certain times to maintain a good sleep schedule? And therefore can this sometimes require you to travel the day before and an overnight stay somewhere?
COMMU-NICATION	• If someone is communicating actions, this should be done in writing. That might involve them sending an email after a conversation to confirm actions. • No meetings/working in places with a lot of background noise. • Make available a way to send voice notes, instead of typing. • When do you want to be contacted and in what way? e.g. emails before 6 p.m., nothing after 6 p.m. • When should something be communicated more urgently? e.g. if there is a change of time less than twenty-four hours before something starts, someone should call instead of email.

Access riders can be as long or as short as you might find useful, and are often very specific to your creative practice. It's about communicating the ideal conditions for you to do your best work. I find that shorter access riders are more effective, as they're often more accessible for the reader too.

TL;DR: Access riders are guides so that other people know what conditions need to happen for you to do your best work.

2.1.6. The argument against access riders

Access riders are great – they're a useful tool for you to articulate your needs. However, when we write things down, something very odd happens.

People can often think that once something is written down, it will never change. But our experience of ADHD can fluctuate based on all sorts of things, from medication dosage to hormonal changes. It made me reluctant to write down what I needed, because it seemed like they worked under the presumption I knew what I needed.

I don't always know what I need. In the same way that this book does not contain the answer to life and the universe for ADHDers, my brain doesn't contain all the information on how it works. Sometimes I just know something is happening in an unhelpful way, and I struggle to understand why or what I need to stop it.

When you're first becoming aware of ADHD, or you're going through a life change or other event, you might not have worked out yet what you need. There is a danger here that if you ask for something that isn't on an access rider, then it feels superfluous to your needs. Some people believe it gives them permission to reject further requests, because we don't know the answer to everything at the start.

There is a risk that access riders can stop feeling like advocacy documents to support an ADHDer, and feel more like contracts that are designed to restrict the scope of needs that an ADHDer can ask to be met.

I don't think this is the default, but it was a concern at the time, and it proved to become true for me in some isolated incidents later on.

If you become aware of new ways your access can be facilitated, then you should be able to add those to your access rider, whatever form it takes. This is something we should be mindful of.

This is part of the reason I decided to have a verbal conversation with people about access, because I find that conversation retains some malleability as opposed to the rigidness of writing something down. A document might work better for other people, but I would rather explain more often and be able to update people, rather than risk something being perceived as static.

TL;DR: Make sure your access rider can change and not become restrictive; how this happens might depend on your process and who you're communicating with.

2.2. Industry skills

2.2.1. Time management

I have been late to things for most of my life. Most of the time I couldn't explain it, I would start getting ready at the right time and somehow always turn up twenty minutes late. I would spend most of my life rushing to places, because I was somehow always running behind.

I have had various 'day jobs' which were not my creative practice, and I became amazing at dreaming up reasons why I was arriving late. There was one summer where I had a bike puncture so often I am pretty certain my manager thought I was cycling over nails on purpose.

This is not uncommon for ADHDers: we are often a bit unaware of time. There is some deeper science behind it, but I think of it as not being very good at noticing that time is passing. Or getting distracted by things and forgetting there is a deadline.

Believe it or not, the answer to this is not just to 'focus harder', as someone once suggested to me.

A lot of the techniques in Part One of this book related to time blindness and creative practice, but I think it extends into the work around your creative practice.

If you're an actor that's always late to castings, or a graphic designer that's always late to client meetings, then it doesn't matter how good your personal techniques are: you might not get the chance to try them out.

The process of combatting this is to identify where you're not noticing time, and come up with some kind of mechanism that creates external accountability. We need to create ways that someone/something else is making sure we get somewhere on time.

1. I know some people find it useful to play the same album of music every morning, starting automatically at the same time. The changing of the songs means there is a reminder of time having reached a set point, and you realise where you should be in your routine. I loved this idea for about two weeks, but then I got bored of the album I chose and it didn't work.

2. I have a rule for myself that before I go to bed, I must get everything ready that I will need for the next day. My bag is packed, my lunch is packed, the things I need for breakfast are in the place on the kitchen counter they always are. It doesn't matter how drunk I am when I get home, I will try to make overnight oats at 2 a.m. after too much gin. This creates a path of least resistance when I am trying to leave the house.

3. This relates to my other rule, which is that I have two of just about everything I need. Before I started doing this, I would have to go and find my phone charger in the morning in case I needed it while I was out. Or I would have to find the sunscreen on days it was sunny. It does mean I constantly carry a bag that's a bit bigger than normal, but it saves me from not noticing the time as I search for my sunglasses.

4. Maybe the most important rule is that if it's not in my calendar, it is not happening. Even if I have a possible meeting that I am waiting to be confirmed, I will put a placeholder in my diary because otherwise I will not remember. If I need to travel between locations, then I put my travel time in my diary so I don't get distracted and leave the first venue late. I put everything in my diary including any kind of morning exercise, social plans, holidays, appointments. This gives me fixed points in time when events and transitional processes like travel must start.

5. Set alarms on your phone for when you need to leave somewhere. I know it looks odd and might be socially awkward, but it's a good disruption that sometimes provokes other people to make sure you're not late too.

6. I leave 'baggage' time in most of the things I do. Normally I assume a journey will take about fifteen minutes longer than it does, to make sure I don't miss a connection. The reality of this is that now I end up arriving about twenty minutes early to everything, but at least then I am not late.

The other side of time management is that sometimes time is not a helpful thing. Sometimes it's important that we are given permission to be late or to turn up at a different time.

The techniques above describe a type of work, and to turn up on time, I am often doing more work than my peers to be there. I often lose relaxation time, because I am leaving earlier to ensure I don't miss a connection. It costs me more to have two of everything and maintain that.

My favourite creative projects to be a part of are those where people can turn up late, and there is no anger or fury, there is just adaptation. In order to do this, it requires us to change our creative process: rehearsals can't be as strictly regimented, they have to be flexible. Meetings can't be packed back to back, making them happen at speed.

This is where the sector needs to exercise some imagination. How can we re-imagine the way we work, so time is not a suffocating energy? This is the real work to be done here.

TL;DR: If you don't notice time passing, create systems where something/someone else does. Or remove the requirement to be on time.

2.2.2. Rejection sensitivity

As part of making *Education, Education, Karaoke* I had to pitch it to different theatres to find some programming slots. Though I am pretty good at pitching other people's projects, I'm not always great at pitching my own. Once I'm emotionally invested in something then I feel very sensitive to the potential rejection.

I don't think anyone likes rejection, but the emotional dysregulation that often comes with ADHD can make it feel very big.

I would talk myself out of pitching the show to various theatres, and despite the fact that I had articulated good reasons, they were definitely attempts not to expose myself to possible rejection.

I began experimenting with ways I could get the play out there without avoiding things, and I slowly found things that did help:

1. One of the best parts of making *Education, Education, Karaoke* is that the director and designer I worked with (Scott Le Crass and Tim Kelly) fully gripped the show and shared the creative responsibility with me. I had originated previous productions where it felt like I held a different responsibility, but Scott and Tim embraced the collaboration to such an extent that it became 'our' show. In this more collaborative model it felt like we were sharing the rejection, and we could support each other in a very intrinsic way. That experience made me notice

how I had always tried to be quite collaborative, often working with a designer from the first draft. It also changed my practice; now I don't even begin working on a project unless I am doing it collaboratively.

2. Your practice might not work in this collaborative way though, so the second thing I found was that if I could find out when the rejection would happen, I could prepare for it. It can be difficult to convince commissioners/producers/directors to deliver a rejection differently, but it can be easier to find out when it is going to happen. In these scenarios I can prepare, make sure I am with a friend who can support me to handle it if needed, or go and do something that allows me to work that experience through my body.

3. I have mentioned this in Part One for different reasons, but it's always a good idea to move between different projects at different draft stages. This means that if you experience rejection, there is a productive action you can take to try and push something else forward instead, while that project has a pause.

But it's not just us that needs to change, it's the way our sector offers 'work'. A lot of creative work that you can apply for, instead of being described as 'labour', is described as an 'opportunity'.

The way it feels like you're winning a prize, as opposed to getting a job, creates a pedestal which makes the fall much higher when you don't get the 'opportunity'. It's important to recognise that the language of 'opportunity' is emotive in a way that creates a more significant feeling of rejection.

There is currently a movement towards competitions and open calls for creative projects, which is not always a bad thing. But at some point, we should consider whether giving 99% of people a feeling of rejection and only 1% a feeling of success is useful for the development of creatives as a whole.

This is especially prevalent in early-career opportunities. We expect creatives to invest emotion, and part of themselves, into an application. We might ask them to talk about how their project relates to their marginalisation. We might ask them to sell us their identity, and how their lived experience features in a piece. These are all, theoretically, important things to ask. But then the majority of applicants are rejected, and we don't take care of the investment we have asked them to make.

There is no neat answer here yet, but I think there is a huge piece of imagination needed to change the culture of this.

TL;DR: Collaboration is an access-support technique to help with rejection sensitivity, and there is a lot of change needed in the sector.

2.2.3. Networking

I don't know if anyone really likes networking. It's a slightly awkward attempt to find some common ground with people you don't know, and there are no real rules on how you should/shouldn't do it.

For me the most difficult part of networking is that I can't always hear people well. As a sector, we tend to put a lot of people in very small rooms, and ADHD often comes with problems with audio-processing. This means I struggle to pick people's voices out of loud background noise; if you add moody lighting so I can't use lip-reading to help, then I really do not know what is going on.

I have perfected the art of reading body language so I can appropriately react to conversations without knowing what has been said. I know which mannerisms require a laugh, a frown or a nod of agreement. Networking in loud environments for me is like durational performance art, and I am not a performer.

This – coupled with all of the social rules I don't do well, like constantly interrupting, or talking too fast, or being distracted by a topic that derails a useful conversation – makes traditional networking a largely pointless activity.

However, if I wanted to be collaborative and work with other people, I had to find ways to meet those people.

For me, the process of developing this show at Camden People's Theatre was about accepting the moments when I found things difficult instead of trying to pretend I wasn't finding it difficult. This is an unmasking process; one where, instead of trying to appear like I was doing networking, I had to learn how to accept it didn't work for me and find a new way.

For each of the challenges I face, I tried to listen to myself and come up with a solution that allows me to blend in, and I also dreamed up a solution that is harder to achieve, but doesn't require me to blend in.

Challenge 1: Audio-processing

How to blend in

Going to networking events in loud environments can prove a challenge for me. If the lighting is good then sometimes I can use lip-reading to help, but if I don't already know someone's accent that can make it challenging too. If it is a loud environment I will always go with a friend, let them know the struggle, and ask them to help me. Either we'll hang out in a quieter area, or the friend will repeat things closer to me if I haven't been able to catch them. This is also something that a support worker could do for you. The other thing I can do, but hate doing, is go to the smoking area. I took one drag on a cigarette when I was about twenty and nearly choked, so I can't smoke, but it is often quieter.

The more difficult solution

If I can avoid it, then I specifically create networking opportunities that are not in these environments. I do more 1:1 coffee meetings with people, than I do large events, because I find them easier.
I will often be honest with people about my audio-processing but this can be challenging. My ears have been tested and there is no physical problem with my ear apparatus, and therefore there is a slight imposter feeling when I bring up audio needs. But suggesting locations to meet that I know are quiet gives me the option of whether I explain further or not.

Challenge 2: Interrupting

How to blend in

I am bad at waiting my turn in conversations. This comes down to a lack of impulse control. For a long time I learned the art of being a quiet observer so I didn't interrupt people, but that meant I wasn't fully participating. Now I have found ways to manage impulses.
If I'm networking in a more desk-based environment I'll take a notebook with me, and as impulses come up I will write them down so I know to come back to them later. This helps me generally follow along with a conversation. If it's not desk-based then I often use a finger-counting system to register that I have had a thought: I count on my fingers how many thoughts I have so I can come back to them later.

The more difficult solution

Sometimes I don't do any of this. I have two collaborators who have ADHD, and when I work with them we all speak over each other in a constant mess. From the outside it seems like slightly rude chaos, but for us we feel incredibly stimulated *and* get to interrupt. This is where it can be useful to be upfront about ADHD – sometimes I just tell people I'm likely to interrupt and that I'm not being rude, I'm just excited by their point.

Challenge 3: Small talk

How to blend in

I am awful at small talk. I will talk to you for two hours without breathing about a very specific subject that's interesting to me at the time, but I cannot pay attention for longer than two minutes if we're talking about the weather. This means if I need to do small talk, I have to either prepare a list of appropriate questions and perform, or make it into a game. For example, the game might be to ask questions to work out which *Simpsons'* character someone is most like. Or sometimes I try to ask questions and try to work out which reality TV show someone would be best on.

The more difficult solution

What I would rather do is network on a subject-specific basis. This means it's not a general session, but people who are interested in a specific topic attend and you get to know each other through that topic. It removes the need for small talk. When I have facilitated networking before, I have asked people to initially talk for one minute about a dream project they would love to work on, if money were no object. Often this triggers something passionate, and gives other people subject-specific things to latch on to.

Challenge 4: Social codes and activities

How to blend in

A lot of this comes down to social codes, which can be difficult for anyone to read. If we're supposed to just talk aimlessly then I struggle to engage, so instead I give myself a task. As a big fantasy nerd I think of them as side quests: things I have to do while doing the actual networking. Side quests can be something like working out how many people in the room did Maths at A-level, so I have something to focus my energy on.

The more difficult solution

This means my favourite kind of networking is one where we are given a task. Networking while playing board games, or while having to collaborate on a task, or teaching as a form of networking are all great. It means you're all working within the social codes of a set practice, and at the same time getting to know each other. This avoids any kind of confusion or miscommunication.

TL;DR: Traditional networking is often inaccessible. You can find techniques to game-ify it, or create networking opportunities that work for you.

2.2.4. Meetings

I would love it if my entire life were creative meanderings, but sadly I do have to do a lot of things that look less like creative work.

Human beings love meetings. I understand why: they can be really effective and let us get away from a lot of typing in emails. The thing is, I would say about 90% of meetings are unnecessary and I struggle to focus through them all.

As I went to meetings throughout the Starting Blocks programme, I began to list features of them that I did and didn't find helpful. Here's my summary:

1. There needs to be a serious reason for a meeting to go on longer than an hour. If it does run longer than an hour, we should think of it as a performance. I prefer it when the focus of a meeting changes frequently and there should be a break at least once an hour.

2. Meetings should not be back to back with other things, but if that is unavoidable then meetings need to finish ten minutes before the next thing, to allow for decompression and preparation. My meds make me quite dehydrated, so I need to fill up my water bottle between most meetings.

3. If a meeting does not have an agenda, it is probably not needed. I know they're very business-y things, but they are also an accountability mechanism and useful for time management to ensure we're getting through everything we need to do.

4. There should be someone who is collecting and distributing actions. Sometimes full notes are necessary for a meeting, but if I'm honest, I rarely read notes properly. I do need to know actions that have been agreed in a summary distributed soon after. Ideally this person should not be someone who also needs to discuss something in the meeting, to avoid multitasking.

5. If the function of the meeting is to share information and not discuss information, it doesn't need to be a meeting. If the function is to share information, then that can be done in a more flexible way when people can engage with it on their own terms. If you need to share information, maybe it all gets written down, and everyone is invited to an optional

body-doubling session to sit and read the information, if that accountability is useful.

6.   If there is pre-reading for a meeting, this must be sent around well in advance. Ideally there should also be an indication of what information in the reading is necessary and what is optional. If possible, there should also be body-doubling time structure before the meeting, or at the beginning of the meeting, to do that reading.

7.   We have lived through a pandemic, we all know how to use a video call. I do not get a thrill from sitting on trains travelling to an in-person meeting – if it can be online then that option should be seriously discussed.

These rules will be different for a lot of people. I think meetings are used to fulfil requirements that can be fulfilled in other ways. The example I gave about using body doubling to distribute information instead of a meeting comes from my observation that sometimes people need an information-sharing meeting for accountability,but actually no discussion happens.

I would rather get on with my creative practice, than spend lots of time in meetings that I have very little interest in. Or I would love meetings that function as accountability for my work.

TL;DR: Meetings are a sticking plaster for lots of needs, and you don't always have to have them. When necessary, meetings need an agenda, to be short, and for someone to note actions.

2.2.5. Fidgets

My housemate at the time had bought some kinetic sand for their niece. It's a small tub with some kind of magic sand that you can sculpt without having to add a lot of water.

Something – I think it was pandemic-related – meant they couldn't travel home to give their niece this present. We thought we might as well make use of the one left in our flat.

Night after night as we watched really important TV like *Naked Attraction*, I would sit with the sand pit next to me and play with it. I liked the feeling on my fingers, I liked that I could make it into shapes and then move it around. Eventually my housemate and I had to figure out a system for who would get to use it at any one time.

This was my first journey into fidgets: little toys to play with that help me focus. I resisted buying anything called a fidget toy for a long time, because it felt childish and I didn't believe it was going to be successful at helping me in any way.

But ever curious, I went to a day of devising and meetings around *Education, Education, Karaoke* and took my millennium ball. If you don't know what one is, you should google it (anyone born between 1988 and about 1996 will know what I'm talking about). I told myself I was taking it because I was making a show about schoolchildren and needed inspiration. When we're faced with embarrassing parts of our life, I think it's common that we allow ourselves to believe certain things to make them easier.

I started to use it in lots of different ways. I would throw it around while trying to think of new ideas to give my hands something to do. I would expand and contract it while sitting in meetings about the project. I would even play with it just for something to do while I was waiting for the next meeting to start.

The problem became that a millennium ball wasn't small enough to be portable, and on one blisteringly hot day in my solo rehearsal room I finally relented and ordered about ten different kinds of fidget toys from Etsy.

I liked a lot of them – they were fun to use and play with. I enjoyed having different ones so I could rotate around once I got bored with certain ones. I also enjoyed the level of focus and calm they gave me.

I didn't love it about a month later when I went to pack my bag and head to the studio and found I had lost every single one I bought. This was a repeated cycle. I would buy a fidget toy, lose that fidget toy, and then find it again about six months later, but only briefly until it got lost again. This wasn't too bad, I was always somewhere in the cycle and in possession of a new one or a re-found one, but it meant I didn't have a choice over the toy.

I resorted to what I always resort to when I lose things: I found a way to attach the thing to my body. I used to lose pens all the time. Now I attach them to myself or my bag; I used to lose my wallet, so I attached it to my bag and added a GPS tracker to it. After losing my fidget toys so often I found the best solution: dangly earrings.

They are not an official fidget toy, but they are very effective. They hide in plain sight and can literally never leave your body.

I use sleeper rings, so I can sleep in them too and then just occasionally change out the charms I have dangling on them. You can buy charms separately, and just hang them on earrings you already have.

You can even buy mini Rubik's cubes, puzzles, or just generally dangly bits that feel nice to touch. Nobody really notices if I am playing with an earring, as it's quite common.

If I have to sit still then I find it incredibly difficult, and I get restless really quickly. But if I can channel that need to fidget into a contained toy then the rest of my body can relax more.

People will find fidget toys in all shapes and sizes, and some might not be fidget toys to start with, like:

- Clicky pens, but prepare to annoy everyone around you.

- Anything with a zip that goes up and down.

- A tongue piercing.

- A water bottle with a top that clicks.

- A spring.

- Lego bricks. I had a pair of earrings with Lego on them for a while but I broke them. It was devastating.

I don't think there's such a thing as a bad fidget toy, but there are some that have consequences that can be more damaging than good.

Over the years I have used various body parts as fidget toys. When I was young I used to let my glasses fall down my nose and then fidget my face to move them back up, as if they were a toy for my face muscles. Even when I stopped doing that fidget, I found it difficult to get rid of the compulsion for some years after.

This is gross but I use my nails as a fidget toy. I don't bite them because my teeth don't line up well enough, but I did pick and tear them when they were long. This is fine but can make your nail area vulnerable to infection, bleeding, and looking generally unpleasant.

Some people use their hair as a sort of fidget toy, but this can go to dangerous levels as excessive hair-pulling can make your hair come out. These are often things we resort to when we haven't chosen another place to put the fidget.

As strange and childish as they might seem, fidget toys are an invaluable way to manage restlessness and try to increase your focus. They don't have to be branded as fidget toys, it's about finding what works for you.

TL;DR: Your fidget toy doesn't have to be a toy – it can be an earring or something else that blends in. Try to avoid body parts though.

2.2.6. Access clash

There is often a false belief that something can be 'fully accessible'. This is aspirational language, but it doesn't really exist. The access needs of different people can sometimes clash, and that's okay.

While creating *Education, Education, Karaoke*, we found that in order to see the text on the screen I needed it to be in very bright and high-contrast colours because I am colour blind. When we invited a performer who was dyslexic to test the show, we realised the colours we chose were not helpful for them. This was a bit of an access clash, and it happens in lots of different ways.

When this began to happen for me, I found it quite intense. It seemed like I was going to have to make a choice about whose access needs I was going to meet, but that's not entirely true.

Firstly, there are sometimes solutions where multiple people can access things in different ways. For instance, in the example above, we could add in a switch that changes the colour palette depending on who is reading.

Theatre can be the most challenging form to imagine people accessing work in different ways, because traditionally every audience member looks through the same proscenium arch at the same picture on stage. But sometimes we forget that art forms can be changed. We often have fundamental beliefs about art that we think cannot be altered, but if they're creating barriers, we should deconstruct them.

If this is not possible, because the systems of the world have created a reality where the necessary technology doesn't exist yet, then don't panic.

As a compromise I think our aim is to ensure two things:

1. **Agency**: By 'agency' I mean we should provide accurate information about the ways in which something is accessible,

with context. For example, you could say that there will be a BSL interpreter at a specific place next to the stage. This shouldn't just be communicated to BSL users – it should be communicated to everyone. Sometimes I find it difficult to focus on a play, because of the movement at the side of the stage, so I can make an informed decision whether to engage, or whether to come on a different night. There is a chronic lack of BSL-accessible performances, and there are thousands of shows I can see without the distraction, so I wouldn't ever consider saying I should be privileged. I'm now resolving that access clash by learning BSL so I can engage with both forms of communication.

2. **Options**: It's incredibly important that access clash doesn't force people with access needs to compete against each other, which often happens because we are not given enough options. If there is only one performance with access features, and it creates an access clash, then that could force competition. The responsibility is not on the deaf/disabled/neurodivergent person to solve this, it's on the people that created the clash. If someone knows access clash is happening, they should make sure they can inform people about an optional way to engage.

I've used the example here of access around watching a show, because it makes what I'm talking about more explicit. But the same applies for needs in a rehearsal room or other creative work environments. Some people might need to have the music incredibly loud to hear it better, but that's often overwhelming for me.

In this scenario it's the responsibility of the director/producer/creative team to provide several options:

1. Imagine a way that both needs can be met.

2. Deconstruct the assumption that only music can help in this part of the show.

3. Use the Agency/Options approach to inform both, give some context, and offer an option of how we can all fully engage with the project.

I want to be clear here, that the options part of this doesn't apply between disabled and non-disabled people in the same way.
I am not suggesting that because something is inaccessible – for example, because it doesn't have step-free access – that you offer a person step-free access to a smaller stage than everyone else and suggest they use that. This is a real example that has happened before.

This is specifically about those moments where there is access clash, not when there is inaccessibility.

I am also not pretending this work is easy. It can be expensive to remove access clash, but I generally find that it is theoretically possible.

TL;DR: Sometimes the needs of different people will clash. We should either find a solution, or ensure that people can access the process in multiple ways.

2.2.7. Collaboration

The biggest thing I learned from making *Education, Education, Karaoke* is that I shouldn't make a show alone. I worked with two incredible collaborators on the project who were so happy to run with their respective elements that I didn't feel like I was at the centre of it all.

Theatre in the UK is often obsessed with having a 'lead artist', which I think largely comes from having a single point of responsibility for the project. British art is also historically obsessed with individual genius, which often means that you have to apply for a project solo and then bring on collaborators later. This is not the ideal scenario for collaboration: often the collaboration is fractured, and one person ends up taking on a lot of responsibility. In theatre this often involves being more financially responsible too.

On this project I had the seed of an idea and I found two collaborators with whom I could share the responsibility for dreaming the project into existence in a way that did not burn me out (as much).

I want to be clear that what we did was different to a profit-share production, where people say they'll split the labour and also the profits. Generally, theatre doesn't make profit, except for some specific scenarios. When it does, it can make a lot of profit, but this is not the norm. Profit-shares are a bit of a false promise and often result in people not being paid properly, which is not an ideal condition to work in. If I am constantly distracted thinking about how I'm going to pay my rent, no number of exercises in this book are going to help me focus.

I had worked with the theatre to create a financial structure that worked, in a way that would guarantee fees for the three of us spread pretty evenly. Then we all sat down, agreed we could make something, and ran with our respective elements.

This created an environment where I could implement a lot of the techniques of Part One without needing to have a support worker of any kind. Scott and I would body double whilst working on the script, often in the pub, but there's no rule for body doubling saying rosé can't be involved.

We slowly learned how to manage sensory input for each other and spot signs of stress or pressure. Scott was incredible at creating accountability structures for me, making me send him drafts and track progress on a spreadsheet. Tim was pretty adept already at working with my chaotic brain because we had known each other for about eight years.

A collaborative model of making theatre removes the isolation, formality and often expensive support systems. I decided after this project I was now no longer interested in being a lead artist, or any other type of isolated practitioner. I want to work collaboratively, which can be challenging as a writer, when traditionally the expectation is that you will turn in a script after not speaking to anyone.

This is why I increasingly tell people I am a theatre-maker, which gives me more permission to work collaboratively in a room, even if the practice I bring is primarily about making a text record of the work.

TL;DR: Working collaboratively can be a part of your access needs – and joyful.

2.3. Support systems and workers

2.3.1. Support systems, e.g. Access to Work

I was sitting in front of my computer screen, writing an application to Arts Council England (ACE) for funding to develop *Education, Education, Karaoke* further. It must have been about midnight already because I had been working at my day job all day, came home to write, then had to get started on the funding application.

My laptop screen was too bright, but I squinted at the screen that was asking 'Do you need support?' My immediate reaction was to say no. I had been a support worker in the past, I had helped disabled people apply for funding, and I couldn't swap sides.

But what if I could? I had a diagnosis from a medical professional as well as a lifetime of experience with epilepsy. I was absolutely justified in admitting that the ACE application process was overwhelming for me.

I probably did need support. But I closed the laptop and went to lie in bed and stare at the ceiling for two hours as some kind of insomnia kept me awake.

Every day for the next week I read the page about getting support with your ACE application, as if re-reading it would help me see something in those words that I hadn't noticed before, or that would help me feel at peace with being the one who needed support.

This is not how words work; they do not change, but sometimes people do. It was enough to read them over and over until I found some kind of meaning in the word 'support' that gave me permission to say 'yes'.

When you're at the beginning of your journey, it's often difficult to accept support. I find a lot of people know what they need deep down somehow, but need someone almost to force them for the first time, so they don't have to take responsibility for asking.

This is totally understandable. I, like so many others, felt that asking for help made me too vulnerable. I was walking around the street able to communicate effectively, get into most buildings, and not experience any explicit ableism because of how I existed. But I was going home and working until 2 a.m. every night because I couldn't manage my brain well enough to get anything done.

It took weeks for me to accept that I had a right to access this support, that accepting support was actually a really important part of my role in the sector. If that offer of support went without requests for it to be taken up, would it continue to be offered? By asking for it, I was helping ACE evidence demand and possibly expand their comms to reach other people that might need it.

Once I overcame that first hurdle, I began searching for all kinds of support across the sector. I wanted to finish working before 10 p.m. so I could get some half-decent sleep.

The sector has a number of different ways that can support you with access. Here are some that you should know about:

1. **Arts Council England**: At the time of writing, Arts Council England (ACE) will pay for you to have a support worker if their application process is not accessible to you. They already have alternative formats such as large-print forms of their guidance, but there are lots of ways in which the application process itself might not be accessible. People with dyslexia might struggle with the use of language, visually impaired people might need support to use ACE's portal, and people with ADHD often need support with things like information overwhelm, task management and prioritisation while putting together an application. As ACE has adopted the social model of disability (more on that later) they do not ask for proof of diagnosis or anything like that – there is more information on their website.

2. **Other funders**: ACE are pretty good at being upfront and open about their access support work, but other sources of funding are not so good. Some large trusts and foundations that you might want to apply to are open to providing support for your application, but don't define the process on their websites. I am guessing this is because they're nervous that everyone will ask for it and it will deplete their funds. Before applying to a funder, you are well within your right to email them and ask for accommodations, whether this be a support worker, an extended timeline, or a pre-application chat to help you understand some material. They might say no, but in my experience, a lot of them are open to trying to support you in some way.

3. **Recruitment processes**: The Equality Act 2010 made it unlawful for an employer to discriminate against job applicants because of a protected characteristic, which can include disability. This includes the recruitment of creatives. Employers are required to make adjustments so they are not discriminating against you when hiring for a job. What this officially includes is probably a question for a lawyer, but anecdotally I find it useful to ask for interview questions in advance so I don't get distracted on the

spot, and I always take a notebook in case I need to doodle or write down things I might forget.

4. **Access to Work**: There is a section later in this book that does a deep dive into Access to Work, but it's important to bring it up here. Access to Work is a programme currently run by the government, or specifically the Department for Work and Pensions, that provides funding for disabled people to access or remain in work. There is very little knowledge of the system in arts organisations a lot of the time, because there are few people who are openly disabled or neurodivergent in senior positions, and even less knowledge of it generally for neurodivergent people. It is relatively clear how some disabled people might need support with work (e.g. a BSL interpreter), but it is less clear how neurodivergent people might need support because we have explored this less. If you work for a large organisation then often Access to Work is done through the organisation and they might have to pay a contribution to the arrangement. If you're self-employed in some way then generally you can have your own arrangement and you don't contribute to the cost. It's important to explore this with organisations – if you've been commissioned or are doing a residency, for instance – and see if they have someone that can support you with an application.

Sometimes the creative sector is bad at offering – or accepting – this kind of support, because we have focused on the process of making art instead of the barriers around it for a long time. But these things are real and you should feel able to ask for and access support. As I will mention later in this book, at the time of publication, Access to Work is under a significant review so this information may change rapidly.

TL;DR: There are formal support systems that exist for you already – use them.

2.3.2. How to work with a support worker

I didn't start working with a support worker formally until after I made *Education, Education, Karaoke*, but I have been subconsciously using one for a long time. Throughout making the show I would always work in the rehearsal room with a dramaturg; this is something I have always done, and really I look back now and see that that person wasn't just doing dramaturgy. I was using them like a creative support worker in order to help facilitate my practice.

You don't have to call people 'support workers', and I appreciate that is sometimes a difficult word to adjust to, especially if you are newly aware of your ADHD. But different roles such as producers, directors and curators can definitely deliver support worker functions for you, if you agree on a way they can make that happen.

Here are some of the ways a support worker helps me, and how they might be delivered by collaborators that aren't support workers:

Support 1: Body doubling

How a support worker delivers it

I talked about body doubling earlier in this book. Your support worker can hold structured body-doubling sessions with you, for specific tasks. For example, we regularly do body-doubling sessions to keep on top of everything, from receipt management to setting up the micro-deadlines and sessions for new projects. I find it useful to do these in a regular cycle, hold the time in my diary, and if we don't need it then that's fine.

How collaborators might deliver it

Solidarity models of support are where a group of people recognise that each one has different needs and they find ways to support each other. It might be that in your production team someone can hold a fifteen-minute body-doubling session at the beginning of the day to deal with any distracting emails. You could get together with your collaborators once a week and do all the tasks that you don't like doing. The key to body doubling with colleagues is to recognise the use of it for multiple people, as well as yourself.

Support 2: Prioritisation

How a support worker delivers it

I use a lot of conscious prioritisation techniques, to decide which parts of projects are more important. A lot of this revolves around talking through tasks out loud and working through certain questions that help me figure out what order things need to be done in. This is a great task for a support worker to help with; they don't need to manage the tasks, they just need to help with whatever system you use to prioritise.

How collaborators might deliver it

If you don't have a support worker you probably have a collaborator who you could call every Monday and talk through what you need to get done for the week, to help prioritise your tasks. Again, work in the solidarity model, and understand what is useful to them as well as to you.

Support 3: Reminding and reflecting on techniques

How a support worker delivers it

Despite the fact that I've written this book, sometimes I struggle with a task and completely forget the technique that I know I can use to solve the thing I am struggling with. This is where a support worker is useful to prompt you and say 'Have you tried x?' to remind you to use the tools you have. Sometimes this is not about memory, sometimes this is about becoming so frustrated that I need someone to stop me for a moment and make me think about something else. Some techniques in this book are more effective when someone else imposes them, e.g. if I want to not write for a day, often a support worker is better at affirming the need for that.

How collaborators might deliver it

I have a friend who is an experienced director, and at the beginning of every rehearsal process, she chats to everyone about what they need best to work in the room. She doesn't always use the language of access, as it can be difficult for some people to use. But then she designs a rehearsal process that works for those people, and doesn't assume it will always be the same. I have seen her use distraction boards, and use warm-ups for emotional regulation, as well as physical warm-ups. In this scenario she can become the person that reminds people of what they need, and affirms that they should go and do it. This is a part of leading a project: knowing what your team needs to make the work you want to make.

Support 4: Time management

How a support worker delivers it

As I talked about before, I am late for everything. I was even born nearly two weeks later than planned. My support worker doesn't manage my diary because I like to know what's happening with my schedule, but we did spend time going through a process where they observed the parts of time management I found difficult, and then we developed a system together for booking things in. This includes times when I don't take any meetings because it disrupts my day, limits on meetings every day, and so on.

Support workers might also create useful interruptions to pull you out of one activity and into another, if you have totally lost track of time.

How collaborators might deliver it

There are lots of time-management apps and systems out there, and they can be really effective. The problem is that you need to know your requirements before you can use them effectively. If you don't have a support worker, it might be useful to keep a diary every time you do a time-management process badly, so that you can go back through that diary and see the reasons why you're not managing things well. You can then use these notes to build a system that works, using one of the apps out there.

Support 5: Note-taking

How a support worker delivers it

As I have talked about in other sections of this book, I rarely take functional notes. If I look like I'm taking notes, it is normally just so I can focus better or remember things for a few minutes. If you're doing this, it's sometimes more effective for other people to take notes. I personally find that anything more extensive than a list of action points from any one meeting is too much and I'll never read them, but those action points are really useful for task management.

How collaborators might deliver it

Again, there are a lot of apps that can take notes for you, and a lot of them are free. You can use them to remember notes, or if I'm going alone, I ask for a recap of actions at the end of the meeting so that I can quickly make sure I have them written down and I don't forget anything we've discussed. I never volunteer as the dedicated note-taker in meetings, and I explain to people that I won't be able to participate if I have to take functional notes.

Support 6: Advocacy

How a support worker delivers it

It can often be very difficult for us to admit that we're at capacity/overworking/tired/burnt out/running over time because we haven't paid attention. It can be a lot easier if someone else advocates for you to accept these needs, so that you listen to them and action them. Having someone confirm what you are feeling seems insignificant, but it can be really important if you're caught up in the middle of a hyperfocus and not quite paying attention to your own needs as well as you should.

How collaborators might deliver it

This person doesn't have to be a support worker. Part of what I have done is slowly introduce helpful language to my friends/colleagues/collaborators so that they are able to recognise the signs that I am not focusing on my needs. I am surrounded by a network of people who now affirm my experience when it happens, and one way to get people to do that might be to share this book with them. We generally use the phrase 'I wonder if...' because it is neither accusatory nor invites any shame into the conversation.

Support 7: Emotional regulation

How a support worker delivers it

Emotional dysregulation can often be a very personal thing, or at least it can feel very personal. Depending on the level of familiarity with your support worker, you might prepare an activity that you use when you are dysregulated. The most effective thing can often be for them to notice what is happening and name it.

The way you then handle it is incredibly varied for a lot of people. Although emotional dysregulation is quite common with ADHD, the ways it presents is where I have found the most variety across all the research I have done. I think this is because the way we relate to our emotions is affected by so many factors, and it's hard to isolate it within one part of ADHD.

Generally I recognise the dysregulation and then have to regulate through my body before I regulate through my brain. This normally looks like doing some kind of exercise, like swimming or cycling. Sometimes it's useful for my support worker to give me permission to change my plan of work for the day, and actively instigates a reassessment of what I was going to do. If I am dysregulated, I will be less productive and I sometimes don't want to admit that.

How collaborators might deliver it

In friendship groups or in collaborations, we often know when someone is dysregulated or a bit 'off'. We can see the prickly spikes in emotions that feel slightly disproportionate to a neurotypical brain.

Without a support worker it is useful if you are around someone who might notice and name what is happening. This often involves telling the people you see a lot how you want to be made aware. You don't want them to snap at you, but you might want it posed as a question to make it softer.

Then, you can always prepare a set of actions that you must do once it has been named. This might involve some regulation, like exercise (specific to me), or it might involve kickstarting the process of replanning your next few days according to your capacity. If it's useful to do this with external accountability, this might be where you begin some of the body-doubling techniques described previously.

Support 8: Practical reminders like meds

How a support worker delivers it

If I am buried in a writing project then I can sit for eight hours and not think about food, let alone taking medication. Hyperfocus can be all-consuming and sometimes you need a person to tap you on the shoulder to take your meds.

How collaborators might deliver it

I underestimated for a long time what it took to break my hyperfocus. A phone reminder doesn't always cut it, unless it's incredibly loud. Normally I need some kind of physical reminder, and my solution to that was to get a smartwatch that can vibrate to remind me about things. It's quite difficult to keep typing a script when your wrist is vibrating. Your practice might need interrupting in a different way, but it often has to be a physical interruption.

Support 9: Comms/inbox management

How a support worker delivers it

Even as a writer I get a lot of emails. Just existing in the theatre sector requires a lot of emails because the places where you find work are so decentralised, you have to be on about ten mailing lists just to hear about some opportunities. Couple this with the regular traffic involved with networking, producing, etc., and suddenly my inbox is overwhelming. When there are so many emails, I dread opening even one in case it is a huge, complex email. You can ask a support worker to be in your inbox and manage it, but I prefer to keep on top of all my communication, so we created a different system. I have a series of folders for different days. I often quickly scan an email and then put it into the folder for the day when I'll reply. It's not in my inbox so it's not adding to the overwhelm, then we have body-doubling sessions where we empty the email folders. It's great to make the amount of communication feel manageable.

How collaborators might deliver it

Here are things I ask of people to cut down on the need to do this:

- If an email is longer than two paragraphs and it doesn't specifically need to be written down – call me.

- If an email is longer than two paragraphs and needs to be in writing, the body should contain any actions and it should link to any big bits of text I can open and read when I want to.

- White space is my friend, don't make it crowded. I love bullet points, numbers, summaries, actions in bold. Visual logic is great.

- Tell me how urgent it is in the subject line before I open it. This way I know if I can file it into a folder for the next body-doubling session without reading it.

Support 10: Creating systems

How a support worker delivers it

At the heart of everything I've written here is a systems approach to having a support worker. When I first started working with mine, I said I didn't want her to manage my inbox for me or do my tedious invoices. I said I wanted us to find systems so neither of us had to do that. This means we spent a lot of time researching things like Calendly to manage my diary or automatic email filing to manage my inbox overwhelm. My support worker oversees these systems, to make sure they're running properly, but it means I am still in control and also that if she's unwell or on holiday, then the system keeps supporting me, at least in a basic way.

This systems approach has been the key to ADHD for me. So much of the admin around my creative practice is automated for me now. I know that if emails fit a certain category, then they go in a certain folder. I know there is a time in my diary when I will check that folder. I don't have to make decisions, and considering ADHD largely affects executive functioning/decision-making, that's been incredible.

My writing is somewhat similar. I know I have a dump list, and then once a week my support worker will make sure I take the ideas off that dump list and put them in the place on a document where they need to go.

How collaborators might deliver it

Obviously, these systems can be created without a support worker. But often we don't know what things can look like, because we have been doing them a certain way for a while.

I didn't realise that some people look at an overflowing email inbox and feel fine about it. I didn't realise that was an option available to me, I have always assumed the point of emails was to overwhelm me. It took working with someone else to see the options available to me.

If you don't take this approach with a support worker, you might do it with a friend or a colleague. You and someone else might keep an eye on each other's system to make sure there's support for each of you. Again, we come back to the solidarity model of support.

Support workers can, within safety and reason, be anything you want them to be. There is no set rule for how this works; the important thing is that you understand what works for you and identify ways for other people to help you get that. It's also important that people reading this book who spend a lot of time around people with ADHD, ask their collaborators what they need to do their best work.

Ultimately, tackling this earlier as opposed to later avoids things getting difficult and tense.

TL;DR: There are lots of ways to work with a support worker, or for other people to fulfil isolated functions of that role.

2.3.3. Do you need dramaturgy?

As I neared the end of the Starting Blocks programme, I did a sharing of the show I made and of the things I had learned during the process. On the back of this, people started coming to me to ask about being a dramaturg for projects being developed by ADHDers. Often these were last-minute requests tinged with frustration, because a specific theatre/producer couldn't get a writer to finish a script.

At first I thought it was quite exciting to be asked to get involved in new projects by big theatres. I would waltz into meetings with notes on scripts, or go to a rehearsal with suggested accessible exercises we could try to unlock a scene. But nobody ever wanted what I was offering.

Part of that might be because my answer to all dramaturgical problems is just to make the text more camp – but it's also because I was being asked to solve a problem that didn't exist.

Generally, in Britain, if there's a problem with a script we call in a dramaturg. This is a very varied title. It can mean a person that gives notes on a script, a person that does research, a person that acts as a provocateur in the room to challenge the process of the director, and many other things. Dramaturgs often have varied toolkits, and they're often very good at highlighting things to be resolved by writers.

But I would be invited into a process where theatres were wanting me to somehow dramaturg something that didn't exist yet. A writer would turn up, normally about twenty minutes late, covered in enthusiasm that I was about to do something magic, or shame because I was the third person that had attempted it.

After a few of these, I went for a drink with one of the writers I had been brought in to work with, and we had a good chat. She told me about how she just couldn't get the script out; she had it all planned in her head but couldn't get it down on paper.

It wasn't that she needed help with the form, structure or content of the thing she was working on. She needed a kind of access support that was still very intangible. The theatre had categorised it as a script problem, and therefore brought in a dramaturg. But really they should have brought in an access support worker.

Due to the newness of access support work for ADHDers and the general lack of awareness of what it might look like to need access, it can be difficult to spot these situations. This is especially true for ADHD creatives that are in the infancy of their awareness and haven't yet learned to identify when they need support, let alone what support they need.

Most ADHD writers need someone to sit with them every day/week and body double until the script is finished. Or they need someone to come in and facilitate some devising to game-ify their ideas. They need someone to come and do the things in this book, and that is not what we often call dramaturgy – it is more like access support work.

In situations where you, as an ADHD creative, are struggling, the organisation you're working with might suggest bringing in a dramaturg/a voice coach/a consultant designer/an acting mentor or any number of functions that are designed for neurotypical creatives.

Your challenge is to spot when this happens, and work out what you actually need. Do you need an accent coach? Or do you need someone to body double with you while you watch the accent videos that seem to have been so effective for everyone else in your cast?

It often comes down to the individual to do this labour, because organisations are not equipped with the contextual knowledge needed to know when access support is appropriate.

Two useful questions I ask myself are:

- Does it feel like this is a productivity issue? More often than not this is about access, not about dramaturgy.

- Can I describe precisely what is happening? If not, I need to be able to do this first before I can make an informed decision on what the creative needs.

With these questions I can begin to untangle the correct support to put in place or to ask for.

TL;DR: We don't always need dramaturgy; we might really need body doubling or some of the access support described in this book.

Education, Education, Karaoke got staged, to half-decent reviews and mediocre audiences thanks to COVID outbreaks and the government refusing to pay train workers proper wages. I had taken a show to production, it had achieved a lot of what I wanted it to achieve, but I was tired.

The day after the show, with the set piled up in the hallway of my Zone 3 houseshare in London, I woke up early because I had to go and work somewhere. I tried to eat some breakfast, but every time I swallowed I could feel my tonsils were swollen and it was difficult.

My body felt tired but I didn't have much of an appetite for breakfast anyway – instead I clung to my coffee with both hands. It was 8 a.m. and it was my second one of the morning. I was hoping it would give me the energy to get out of the house.

My brain generally swings between two modes: one which is avoidant of most stimuli, where the bees are asleep and don't want to be disturbed, and another where they are a little bit too awake and will not calm down. On that day they were neither; they were swimming in honey.

Some people call it 'brain fog', but I think there is a gloopiness to it, whereas fog is a cold and brittle experience that often wakes you up. Honey is sticky and seems to trap you in a perpetual state of slow-moving unawareness.

I knew what was happening, but my brain was refusing to look at the words that were hiding in there. Instead I tried to put on my trainers and leave, but I hadn't checked I had everything in my bag. Jumping over the boxes in the hallway, I tried to find what I would need, but my laptop was nowhere to be found. Digging through boxes, it turns out it was in my bedroom upstairs, but the charger wasn't with it. I found that in the boxes, but then I knocked some over while looking. I wanted to leave them, but I knew my housemates would be home before me and they would be in the way. Actually, even if they hadn't fallen over they would probably have been in the way and I should probably have moved them. As the prospect of rearranging the hallway emerged in my head, I knew I would be late to where I was going.

I sent texts to my housemates apologising for the mess and explaining that I was having to dash to work and I would clean it later, but as I stepped out the door I realised there was no key in my pocket. I looked at the hallway full of stuff I had committed to leaving, having just exposed my inability to manage it all to my friends, and I started to cry.

No matter what I had done – the coffee, the prioritising, running around for my laptop – I was going to be late.

Being late can be a minor experience for a lot of people, but as I faced a set piled high, I felt the frustration of every other time I had tried to leave the house. There have been hundreds, if not thousands of times, where I have tried to leave the house and something has prevented me. It feels like someone is playing a trick on you: you know logically the keys are in the house, but you cannot retrieve the memory of where.

Normally I can manage this, but not when I'm burnt out. That was the truth of it: I was crying because I was so burnt out from trying to make the show.

The first signs of burnout for me are always my tonsils; if they're swollen with no other viral symptoms then I know I've gone too far.

It's not easy to admit that you've reached your limit when you're trying to dream into existence a creative project that requires you to keep driving that project forward.

This is the trap of creative work a lot of the time: there is little stability and it often depends on individuals having a lot of drive and tenacity. You have to want to write with everything that comes with that – you can't just want to be a writer.

I don't want this to feel like I'm arguing that all artists must be tortured bohemians with awful lives, as I don't think that's true, useful or productive. Some of the things that come with being a writer are acceptable discomforts. I think it's helpful for writers to have a heightened level of self-awareness, because there is nothing worse than a script where you can see a lack of self-awareness in the writer. This is sometimes uncomfortable and requires some personal emotional work, but I think within the boundaries of a fair expectation.There are some things that are not acceptable but common in other industries so we understand them, like the unstable rates of pay. Generally, as a writer, you are either making less than minimum wage, or you 'make it big' and suddenly make a lot of money. There are few writers that sit in a comfortable medium. This pay structure shouldn't be like this, but it's something that we know going in. I knew and accepted that I wouldn't be going on lavish holidays for a long time.

Then there are the things that are often a reality, but that I didn't know going in. This is the enduring old boys' network in theatre, abuses of power that are covered up, rampant nepotism, no structural way of properly distributing resources, etc. These issues should not exist and are not talked about enough.

Burnout is so high in the creative industries because of the vast number of things that are unregulated. There is an argument to say that we benefit from this – that art requires freedom – but I think we are at our most creative when our other basic needs are met.

I am not going to write a great play while I'm worrying about where my rent is coming from.

Throw ADHD or various other neurodivergence, marginalisations or needs into the mix and it is amplified.

That day I cried, I probably cried for nearly an hour. I cancelled everything. I was so angry at my brain. That can be a strange experience because often we are angry at external things, but with ADHD we are often angry with our own brains.

It takes a long time to really heal from a burnout experience, and an ADHD brain isn't always prone to rest in the same way as we are often taught to rest. We get taught that meditation and yoga are good for us, but we are also taught that in order to access their benefits your brain must be quiet. I find it difficult enough to get my brain to do basic tasks, let alone quieten the bees.

I spent weeks at half-energy. I couldn't just stop because I needed to pay my rent, but I existed purely to survive while I tried to recover. As some clarity began to emerge in my brain – and the bees cleared out the honey – I began to wonder what self-care looked like for me.

This brought into focus the tension that now runs through this book. Would self-care stop me getting to this place again? Or would I simply spend money on scented candles but still exist within a system that is increasingly incompatible with my brain?

This slowly formed into the premise of a show I began to make, which was originally called *Self-care for the Hyperactive Anti-capitalist, or, How to Start a Revolution*. I made it as part of the CRIPtic programme, which is an incredible incubator for disabled, neurodivergent and deaf creatives, and it was performed at the Barbican Centre in 2021.

The premise was that I was going to try different kinds of self-care, and see if they worked for me. I had done so much learning about what I needed professionally, but I had to grow my techniques for getting what I needed in the rest of my life if I was going to stand any chance of sustainability as an ADHD creative.

Part Three is the story of how, while I made a show about self-care, I took the opportunity to learn about the things I needed outside of my professional life to be a creative, to avoid getting to the point of burnout again.

3.1. Caffeine and stimulants

Sat in a university library when I was eighteen, I was trying and failing to write an essay. A lot of time in my first year was spent in a strange class crisis, as it was the first time in my life where most of the people in my environment were middle-class. I vividly remember being corrected on pronunciation a lot, because I had read a lot of words but never had a reason to say them out loud.

Having very few reference points for working-class writers, I fluctuated between heavy assimilation and total rejection of fitting in. One day I would go to a second-hand clothes shop and buy an oversized knitted sweater in ridiculous colours, the next I would change my mind and I was back in a hoodie.

When I found myself inspiration-less in the library, I decided I wanted to feel more literary. I had my best knitwear on, a satchel which didn't have a sports brand down the side, and a view over the lake at my university. I vividly remember going to the canteen and ordering the first cup of coffee I had ever had in my life, because if I knew anything about literary figures like writers, they were always in coffee shops.

I am not lying when I say I started drinking coffee because I thought it would make me more literary. I hated the taste; I don't think

I finished a cup for about three months but I persevered until the caffeine really started taking effect.

Back then I wasn't aware of my ADHD, I used to say my brain was 'fizzy' a lot. Generally anything brain-related was chalked up to being distantly caused by the epileptic seizures I had for about ten years of my childhood. I began to notice that I felt a lot less 'fizzy' and distracted when I drank coffee, and I accepted that this was why people drink it.

Years later as I began making *Self-care or…* I was probably drinking about five cups of espresso coffee every day. My dentist hates me for it, but more importantly my stomach hates me for it. If you've never had a coffee addiction, I'll let you go and research what coffee does to your stomach.

I couldn't function in the morning without at least two cups of coffee before I left the house, and by the time I got to work or a rehearsal room I would want another one. I wouldn't be able to focus without drinking one, but weirdly it didn't make me buzzed, it made me very calm.

I had been diagnosed with ADHD years before making this show, but I had chosen not to take medication. Most ADHD meds are stimulants, and they can lower the trigger threshold for seizures, and I had enough of those for a lifetime in my childhood. I had agreed with my doctor I was going to try and work it out without meds, and I did for years.

Eventually, after learning a lot of what I have written in this book, I realised there were things I couldn't crack. The techniques listed here are often just ways to avoid the harm the world can do to you. They don't stop the world trying to do that harm.

When I had exhausted everything else, I decided to try medication. On the first day I took it I went from having five cups of coffee every day, to wanting none.

The thought of drinking coffee made me feel a bit sick. Luckily, I was a lot more secure in my identity and I wasn't relying on it to make me feel literary any more. But I was relying on it as a stimulant.

I spoke to my doctor about this, and they explained that caffeine, like ADHD meds, is a stimulant. Often, people with ADHD use other stimulants to self-medicate in some way. That's why there is a higher incidence of drug use in people with ADHD. The seizures and a deep fear of their return had stopped me ever taking drugs of any kind, but we don't think of caffeine as a drug.

I had unsuccessfully tried to give up caffeine for a long time, and it never worked. Now I see that my brain had developed a reliance on it that ran deeper than needing to be awake in the morning, I was self-medicating for a condition I didn't know I had.

I used to say that coffee made me sleepy, but that wasn't entirely true. What it was probably doing is the same thing as my meds do for me now, it was (in a weaker way) calming the bees just long enough for me to get some peace and focus on sleep.

This is an important story to understand so I can write about medication more generally. Medication is not a magical solution to everything, and we often find less 'medical' ways to meet our needs and exist in a world that is not built for our brains. These things often hide in plain sight, and can range from picking your nails to disguise a fidget, to drinking five cups of coffee before you can start a task.

I had been incredibly nervous to take medication for lots of reasons, including a fear that it might affect my creativity. What if I suddenly started making work differently or experiencing emotions differently, which shaped my writing? If I learned anything from this experience it was that I had already been medicating in some way, and coffee wasn't having a profound effect on my writing other than making sure it got finished.

Be aware of the ways in which you might be self-medicating. This is not something everyone does, but I have seen it often in ADHD creatives.

TL;DR: Sometimes we self-medicate. It's important you are aware when this is happening, and always remain in control.

3.2. Medication

Sitting on the tube on my way to a rehearsal room, I opened my laptop and began calmly to write at a medium pace. I didn't notice as people sat next to me, I just continued writing calmly. The tears started to fall about three minutes later, as I realised how quiet it was.

It wasn't really quiet, the tube was as loud as it always is. But I had never known that the 'fizziness' in my brain could disappear to this extent. Part of me was sad because an experience I had always known was suddenly lost to me, but I also felt such a sense of peace for that journey.

I had taken ADHD meds for the first time twenty minutes before. I had a friend who has been on meds for years and when I texted them to say how quiet it was, they said they had been waiting for this text. I think it's an experience that is told so often now that it's almost a cliché, but it had a profound effect on me.

My decision to take meds was my own. And it followed after the implementation of most of the strategies in this book, for the practical reason that I was nervous it would trigger epilepsy, not for some ethical belief that medication should be a last resort.

I am writing this book not too long after a TV programme in the UK looked into the way ADHD meds are prescribed. It feels like a hot topic right now, and fraught with a lot of danger, but I think it's important to understand how we sit in relation to medication.

As I have tried to articulate in this book, ADHD is not necessarily a medical condition that imposes restrictions on you. ADHD is, at least for me, a way my brain operates that is increasingly incompatible with the world around us.

That is why I named the Barbican show *Self-care, or, how to start a revolution*, because the ideal form of self-care for me was just to dismantle all the things in the world that make my life difficult. That goes for ADHD as well as other things. I would much rather that people stop being homophobic, instead of doing the therapeutic work I've done to give myself the resilience needed to ignore it.

In a perfect world, when I was diagnosed with ADHD there would have been widespread systematic change in my life. I would have been supported with therapy to deal with a late diagnosis, coaching, changes to the structures in my life such as work; basically all of the things that would remove the barriers I face in the world. In fact, when we began to identify the first ever person with ADHD, the ideal would have been that we nudged the structure of the world slightly to make it possible for all people with ADHD to experience a level of comfort. This goes for lots of neurodivergence and disabilities: when we invented the wheelchair it would have been amazing if we just automatically started using ramps or stopped building stairs.

This magical solution is not so simple though, because the world is big and complicated and our economic systems don't exactly focus on empathy for people. Our contribution to society is often measured by our productivity, a metric which is incredibly different for disabled/deaf/neurodivergent people most of the time.

We might have hoped that when I had suspicions about ADHD I was offered a timely assessment by the NHS, which included looking at other aspects of my life. Some symptoms of ADHD can be the product of things like PTSD, and this kind of holistic assessment might have given me a greater understanding. Then, there would have been state support to access the therapy/coaching/workplace adjustments to holistically support the different ways my needs could exist.

Unfortunately, in the UK, a systemic underfunding of the NHS has left urgent life-threatening care on its knees, let alone holistic care for neurodivergence or mental health that don't have any urgent markers. There is not the resource or the understanding to do any kind of holistic treatment of ADHD properly, unless you curate it yourself and pay for it.

In the absence of any of this, we are left largely with two things:

1.   Community-gathered coping mechanisms, like this book.

2.   Medication, which is normally achieved at first through some partially private means.

Without any kind of financially accessible holistic approach, the most cost-effective way for us to support ourselves is often medication. It does not tackle all aspects of ADHD, but generally it helps with a very broad range of problems, which at least makes working in the current labour market and supporting ourselves a bit more viable.

Medication is not magic. Medication cannot replace the therapy I have done relating to my late diagnosis, but it can help me achieve the level of focus necessary to work effectively and pay my rent.

I do suspect that elements of my life which are often attributed to ADHD might also be attributed to other things. For example, I think my therapist and I agree that I am particularly ill-equipped to deal with emotional dysregulation because of other things that have happened to me. It would be nice if at the point of ADHD diagnosis, I had been supported to find this out, in order to be more specific with treatment, but it doesn't lessen the effectiveness of medication.

As it was, I was trialled on medication via a private clinic and then handed back to the NHS for ongoing prescriptions, and that was the extent of the involvement of the NHS.

The hostile environment that currently exists around ADHD medication is focusing on some of what happens in private clinics. I do think this is bad; I think the benefit of the NHS is not only that it's free, but that we can have some sense of standardisation and oversight over what its workforce are doing. I don't think individuals should be forced into private healthcare systems in order to get the support they need.

But there is no other option right now. Until there is a fully functioning NHS and a holistic approach to neurodivergence that seeks to address a wide range of needs in patients, as opposed to making the problems go away, it is dangerous to remove the one effective support system that is available to people.

Our focus should not be on looking at how bad the current system of diagnosis and care is, and making documentaries criticising it. Our focus should be on looking at how good a fully developed system *could* be, and creating documentaries about how we move towards that model. This might also include criticism of the current system.

The decision of whether to take medication or not is yours. It is not a necessity; I achieved a lot without medication, but it was expensive. I was on some creative development programmes at the time and used the grants I received to pay for coaching and therapy, but this is not a dependable way to find support, particularly at a time when financial pressures mean there are fewer programmes like these (indeed the ones I participated in no longer exist).

It might feel like medication is your only option. It is not, but it might be one of the only financially accessible options right now, depending on how the world is structured.

Don't feel pressured into taking medication, but also there is no shame in taking it. I take it knowing that if there was a change in the world I would stop, but I feel no shame in taking it until that happens.

This is how I get through work days and make sure my rent is paid. There is no point to all the other stuff if I can't do the basics of making enough money to live.

TL;DR: Medication is not the only option, but it might be the only financially accessible option right now (until the revolution).

3.3. Access to Work and why it might be useful

I was diagnosed with ADHD as an adult, and I had very little experience of people supporting me, especially financially. Of all the types of neurodivergence I feel like the one that had the most visibility for me was dyslexia. I knew a few friends who had received software or technology to help them through university. I had for a long time understood myself as someone who didn't fit into that category of need.

I had held down (ish) jobs for a while, but I had struggled massively. I don't think I had done any one role for longer than six months, as I inevitably found aspects I couldn't do well or parts that I didn't find motivating and I moved on to something else. When someone suggested to me I should try 'Access to Work' after I was diagnosed with ADHD, it took about eighteen months for me to really look into it properly. But I figured it had to be part of the exploration of care I was doing while making my new show.

I had no context as to what support would look like for me, and needed to do a lot of work coming to terms with the knowledge I had acquired about ADHD, to understand myself as someone who might be worth supporting.

'Access to Work' is a programme that is run by central government, that provides grants and funding to people with health conditions/disabled people to access or remain in work. It is an incredible thing to exist, though it doesn't exist without its problems. The administration involved is relatively intense and there has been widespread criticism of the decision-making process.

There are a lot of guides online about the practical aspects of applying to Access to Work, so I'm not going to cover that. But I do think I can do some myth-busting and guiding for people with ADHD, so this programme feels like something that can be more easily understood.

1. **You are worthy of support**: There is not enough knowledge around ADHD for there to be a widespread understanding that it can require support. It has been characterised as 'naughty young boys' for such a long time that we often struggle even to conceptualise it as something that exists in an adult workforce. Without a broad understanding, it can feel isolating when advocating for support for yourself if you suspect other people don't understand why you are doing it. But you are worthy of that support; it is not your fault that there is a lack of knowledge and understanding.

2. **Examples of things you might be offered**: It can be difficult to imagine what you might ask for. In my experience, the person that did my 'workplace assessment', where they consider what you might need, was incredibly affirming and really nice. They often bring up things that may help you, but there are also things you can commonly ask for.

   - **ADHD coaching**: You can work with someone to help you create access systems. I had done a form of coaching previously, so I didn't choose to do this.

   - **Software**: There are task-management programs or notation software that can support you. If a premium subscription is required to access them, then it is something you can discuss in your assessment. For creatives, you might need to help them understand why you need the software.

- **Hearing support**: There are special hearing aids you can get that help you to identify an individual voice in a loud room or pay attention to a specific person. Access to Work can provide these, but often require you to have a letter from the NHS saying they don't provide it.

- **Support worker**: A support worker can help you with inbox management, time management, overwhelm, whatever it is in your practice that is inaccessible. You often need to tell them how many hours per week you would need, and what they would be doing, so it might be worth thinking about this in advance.

- **Hardware**: There are different electronic devices they can provide for you, in order to do your work better. For example, there are certain writing tablets that are really useful for writers with ADHD and might be necessary for your job.

- **Anything else**: Outside of office work it can be difficult for them to properly conceptualise what your job looks like, so it might take some research to make sure you can explain it, and explain why you need certain things. It's important you do this advocacy; it is easier to reduce your grant in future, but generally more difficult to increase what they are providing you with.

3. **Managing an Access to Work grant**: Managing the grant itself is quite inaccessible, especially for someone with ADHD. Your exact arrangement can vary, but there is usually some kind of reimbursement form with invoices attached. You might want to factor in an hour a month, or something similar to that, into the support worker time you need, in order to make sure this

happens effectively. I have generally found them understanding of this.

At the time of publication, this information is correct, but the Access to Work scheme is under significant review, and it is quite challenging to predict what it will look like in the future. You should check the most up-to-date information before beginning an application.

TL;DR: Access to Work is not an easy process, but it exists for you, and it can be useful.

3.4. Social model and the word 'disabled'

Imagine it is the early 2000s. I'm sat in an office that smells like cleaning products and has second-hand toys everywhere. A doctor looks at me, slightly puzzled, and asks me, 'Do you understand what happens if I write this on a piece of paper?'

A future of driving flashed before my eyes and was lost, that's the thing the doctor said was most important. Now, I didn't care about cars, but I was pretty convinced I was going to fly a spaceship at some point. That is the future I will miss, but my parents are pretty scared of what is happening to me so I think it must be a scary thing too.

'Yes, I understand,' I say as the white-clad astronaut I imagined drifts off into outer space never to return to any part of my reality.

The doctor doesn't turn back to my parents. He always speaks directly to me, allowing my parents to add things if it's useful. 'Don't treat him like he's Disabled, he should have a normal life,' he says, really more to them than me, but I think he is always watching for my reaction. I rarely meet his gaze, I am scared he'll see something else in my head as well as the epilepsy.

I am not Disabled, I am normal. To have that thought inserted into your mind aged eight, when your world is already being turned upside down, is quite powerful. For the next ten years my life was restricted, I slept in a bed with a special monitor that would set off an alarm in my parents' room if I had a seizure while asleep. I arrested in my first seizure and might have experienced SUDEP (Sudden Death in Epilepsy) if an off-duty fireman hadn't been camping near us in Scarborough and performed CPR on me. This story is a whole separate show that I made years ago.

Despite this, I would have seizures in the morning and then go to school, albeit a little late, but I never had a proper day off once I was on meds and my seizures calmed down. It was so important to the doctors and everyone else that I was 'normal', and so it became important for me too.

As I became an adult, I found myself supporting other creatives that were 'Disabled' and I saw my role as the 'normal' person supporting someone. When I was diagnosed with ADHD I was unsure of the word 'Disabled' at first, as there was such an intrinsic part of me that had been taught to resist that word. It felt as if I was occupying space that wasn't for me: a space that people who experience immense and profound barriers to their basic safety and wellbeing should be occupying.

I don't remember who told me this, but I was reminded as I got older that 'disabled' is a verb: to disable something or someone. It is not a descriptor based on things you can see about a person; it is a neutral description of a fact. This is a grounding principle of the social model of disability for me, which says we are not disabled by our 'impairments', but by the ways in which society creates barriers for us. If society was built differently, that verb wouldn't be used, because society wouldn't be disabling us any more.

A professional footballer who has run around their entire career and competed in the World Cup might break her leg. Then, temporarily, if she were using a wheelchair, she would be being disabled by the number of buildings that do not have step-free access. Then, once recovered, that person probably wouldn't be disabled any more.

Disabled is not an aesthetic identity designed to elicit pity; in fact pity is a really unhelpful feeling for disabled people. Disabled people have the potential to live full lives according to their experience of the world, and having pity for them doesn't dismantle the barriers that are stopping them achieving what they want.

Accepting the factual use of the word helped me access spaces which are often populated with other disabled people. It is only recently that neurodivergent people have identified with the disabled community, and there are still a lot of variances around this. However, there is a growing understanding that more disabled people means more people that can act in solidarity to help each other and to justify changing inaccessible structures in the world. It is useful for more people to identify as disabled.

There is some nuance to this. For example, disabled is not a catch-all term. There are people who prefer to identify as neurodivergent or deaf, as opposed to disabled, for incredibly important cultural reasons. I entirely reject hierarchy within disabled people, but I do recognise that I hold a certain amount of privilege in the sense that I rarely experience profound physical barriers to accessing space. Nor do I experience the level of communication barriers some BSL-users face when most of the country's population hasn't learned BSL. I am conscious of not dominating space and conversation because of this privilege, but I have made peace with the term 'disabled'.

The level of productivity expected of me, the social expectations of timekeeping, loud or overstimulating environments, and all the things described in this book: these are the structural fabric of our society that disables me.

Once I became comfortable with that, I managed to access communities of creatives that were interested in thinking deeply about the ways in which we can change things in order to help each other. I am now learning BSL because of the number of deaf collaborators I have, and I work entirely in 'relaxed' environments because of the number of neurodivergent collaborators I have.

Accessing this kind of community and mutual support has been a fundamental part of good wellbeing for me. It has allowed me to better advocate for my needs, understand the validity of those needs, and access emerging information about techniques that might make my life easier and my creativity richer.

It is the only way I could make *Self-care, or, how to start a revolution*. That artist development programme was for disabled artists, and I met people there like Jamie Hale, whose art is an endless source of inspiration for me. I couldn't have felt comfortable in that space, without first understanding how I could fit into it in a way that was respectful and right.

TL;DR: Use 'disabled' as a verb. It does not need to elicit pity; it might be a starting point for building a community.

3.5. Diagnosis

'Clear your mind and breathe out', the instructor softly said, as I attempted to raise my arms above my head. 'Hold still with your arms raised,' she said, so gently it barely existed in the room. I peeked one eye open to see if she was really standing still and relaxing. She was, it was real.

I felt nothing but an intense desire to move and fidget, and an absolute inability to clear my mind in the ways she was describing. I had started learning about yoga with my friend Sally Lofthouse as part of the process of making the show, I was trying out different self-care ideas. It went like this:

TOM   When is the next move?

SAL   Soon, just breathe out again for me.

TOM   Sal, I need to move.

SAL   Bring your arms down and relax.

TOM   What do I do while I'm here?

SAL   Nothing, just be still in order to relax and feel the ground beneath your feet.

TOM   Are you kidding me?

SAL   This will help you focus.

TOM   I feel like I'm about to explode.

Sal and I tried just about everything there was to get me to like yoga, but ultimately, I felt it was trying to make me assimilate into very neurotypical social codes. Versions of yoga practice are often used in acting rehearsals as warm-ups because they help actors 'ground' themselves and find a sense of stillness.

On another project I was working with an actor who recognised that the breathing exercises and yoga done at the start of rehearsals had always been difficult for them. They were naturally fidgety and never particularly quiet in their mind – just like me. They had in fact always suspected that they had ADHD, but had been nervous to pursue diagnosis.

These sorts of conversations happened a few times. It's amazing that as soon as you begin to externalise your experience of the world by talking about it, other people suddenly realise they're being given a way to understand the confusing feelings they have always had. This is part of the reason why ADHD awareness on TikTok has been so effective. We experience struggles which we don't have the words to explain, and suddenly one of the biggest social media platforms in the world was awash with language that could help us.

The general pattern is that someone starts to ask me a lot of questions. Then they ask for book recommendations, just to 'understand' it better, then they secretly ask me if they should get diagnosed. I'm not entirely interested in diagnosis for my practice; I work on the principle that if you tell me something as part of an access need, I'm not going to ask you for the doctor's note to justify it.

Diagnosis is incredibly hard to access in the NHS: waiting lists are very long, and I have observed a culture of trying to avoid diagnosis. You can choose to use a shared care agreement where the NHS will refer you to a private diagnosis pathway, but this can be tricky to confirm and very expensive. Also, if you consider the previous section about the dominance of private healthcare in ADHD and the lack of oversight there, a diagnosis of ADHD can (on rare occasions) be looked on questioningly by the NHS. The diagnosis process for ADHD is complicated anyway. You can observe the presence of seizures and certain brain patterns to diagnose epilepsy, for example, but ADHD is usually entirely diagnosed on collections of symptoms.

I think diagnosis is too unstable and inaccessible right now for me to advocate everyone pursues it. But that said, it can be useful.

For example, you require a diagnosis to apply to Access to Work if you would like them to fund adjustments in your work life. You require a diagnosis in some more traditional work environments to justify the request for accommodations, especially in an arts sector strapped for cash and desperate to cut costs anywhere. A diagnosis can be a useful advocacy tool, that gives you the confidence to advocate for your needs, because then you're backed up by something medical.

But I think this medical over-reliance is probably not the most useful thing in the long term. It's important that society begins to adopt the social model of disability more, where people don't have to constantly provide doctors' notes to justify the help they so obviously need.

The argument that's usually made about accessible diagnosis is that eventually everybody will be diagnosed with something. Which in a sense seems like a bad thing, but is it? If we accepted that most people find the world challenging in some way, and also adopted some solidarity principles instead of intra-community competition, then we would quite swiftly begin to change the world's structures, because we could see that they are incompatible for the majority of the population.

Whether you're diagnosed or not, if the techniques in this book and others are useful, you should use them. Don't wait for a diagnosis to find structures that help you.

TL;DR: Diagnosis shouldn't be necessary for you, but it is often practically necessary for existing in the world.

3.6. Non-medical support

'How has your week been?' my therapist would ask me through a computer screen. It was always my least favourite question, because I couldn't really recall anything interesting that had happened, until we got about three months into sessions and I began to understand the question.

It wasn't really about giving an accurate account of all my week, but a method to look at some surface behaviours. When I knew I was going to explore wellbeing, I knew part of it was going to have to include therapy. I had already started it before this project; ADHD is not the biggest thing that has happened to me in my life and there was already other work to be done.

But as I got diagnosed, it was something that we discussed at length.

I had the specific experience of being diagnosed as an adult, after the majority of my life to that point had been controlled largely by something else that originated in my brain. Everything vaguely brain-related was put down to epilepsy. When I began describing myself as 'fizzy', people would talk about how a lot of people with epilepsy also have anxiety. By the time I got my ADHD diagnosis I was left feeling like a whole version of my history had been obscured by the frantic panic around another diagnosis. I felt a sense of loss at what my life could have been if I had known earlier.

I thought of everything, from the time I totally missed an A-level exam and the improved grade I might have received, to all the time I had wasted daydreaming and frantically trying to catch up with everyone else.

This sense of loss, at the past that could have been, is not entirely uncommon among friends who became aware of ADHD in their adulthood. There are lots of other feelings that are often prominent following an adult diagnosis too. The important thing is that we recognise that there is a need not only to deal with the current symptoms of ADHD, but also the less tangible things that medication can't touch. These are things like how your ADHD has affected your relationships, friendships, achievement, happiness, sex life, anything.

The world is still a somewhat hostile place for a person with ADHD. We often spend a lot of time closeted and not telling people directly about our needs, at least at first. Whilst there is a widespread understanding of the detrimental effects of being closeted and queer, there is not one for neurodivergence. It is largely overlooked, but the same feeling of shame and low self-worth can often manifest.

Medication and coping techniques might help you avoid future experiences of these feelings of shame, but they won't entirely address your past experiences of them. You still have to come to terms with the feelings you are having around any kind of diagnosis.

I am not advocating that everyone goes to therapy when they become aware of ADHD. Therapy is expensive and largely inaccessible to many people, and the six sessions of CBT that is the NHS 'cookie-cutter answer' to most things is woefully inadequate in my opinion.

Though therapy is financially inaccessible, it's worth considering the ways in which you might access some kind of therapeutic practice to begin recognising and interpreting these internalised feelings. I find that engaging in therapy makes my creativity better. I am more aware of where I am inserting myself into a piece, and can do it with more specificity and subtlety. Sometimes the act of being creative can be therapeutic; sometimes you get lost in writing and characters say things that jump from your unconscious without you realising.

When I was writing the final version of *Can You See into a Black Hole?*, I found myself working on an ending that I never intended to write. I was so engrossed with what I was writing, and suddenly found myself writing the protagonist's words: 'It wasn't my fault.' It was about 11 p.m. the night before my deadline, but I realised that the character had realised the things I also needed to realise.

The sense of self-awareness gained through therapeutic practices can't be found in a box of medication. To some extent, your psychological history can make it hard for it to be effective. If you're taking medication which helps you focus, but you constantly become emotionally dysregulated by a specific stimulus and don't understand why, then upping your meds isn't going to solve that. Figuring out what is *really* happening might give you a better chance.

Even if you don't feel comfortable doing any kind of deep exploration, the baseline useful thing to do is make sure you're not dealing with too much internalised ableism. To use myself as an example, I've talked about the binary between 'normal' and 'disabled' that was instilled in me when I was young and vulnerable, and (though less so now) this still plays a big role in my ability to advocate for my needs. I still find myself feeling shame when I am trying to ask rightfully for something that I need. There is still a reminder of that longing to be 'normal' that was impressed upon me for so long. This is a form of internalised ableism. We often have a better knowledge of things like internalised homophobia because I think it has been written about more, but internalised ableism is important too.

Things you might do to care for your emotional needs are:

1. **ADHD coaching**: There are ADHD coaches who can support you to think through non-medical things you might want.

2. **ADHD talking groups**: There are talking groups you can find, where you can chat to people with a similar experience, and this can often help you process your thoughts.

3. **Reading about other experiences**: There are books that go deep into this aspect of ADHD, with a lot of exercises and anecdotes that can be helpful. There are books that look more generally at internalised ableism too.

This is what I mean by a holistic approach to ADHD in the earlier sections: we shouldn't be reliant on a single support mechanism to address all of our needs.

TL;DR: Make sure you're meeting your historical emotional needs, as well as your current creative needs.

3.7. Friendships/relationships

We often underestimate our personal relationships when we think of creativity. But humans have a lot of different needs, and it's unfair and possibly quite damaging to expect our creative practice to meet all of those needs. Generally people need friends and relationships, or at least other humans to meet some of their needs.

Personal relationships are important because that life experience feeds into our creativity. These relationships are normally with the people who care for us and who ensure we can decompress properly. They are also a huge part of spotting when we have gone too far, and telling us we need to take time off.

My impulsiveness and my inability to fit into some social situations has made it difficult to make and maintain friends sometimes. I know it's something we're not supposed to say, but it is true. I'm probably better at bonding with colleagues in jobs, where you're not required to have as deep a connection, because I can use a 'performed' version of myself to make friends with them. My genuine self is sometimes a little difficult to get along with.

In my experience, people with ADHD often flick between being over-committed/drained out and being isolated/somewhat lonely. This is not true for everyone, but there is a certain amount of chaos that can follow us around.

Part of maintaining relationships is that they require honesty, they can benefit from you opening up about having ADHD; then people can empathise with your constant interruptions and emotional outbursts. This is not a suggestion that you should wear a badge, but I do think friends might have a greater understanding of things that can annoy them if they understand what is happening for you.

There is also a running joke that neurodivergent people subconsciously migrate towards each other. I don't know that there is any science behind it, but I do have a group of friends where we all met because we are creatives with ADHD, and we have a high tolerance for speaking to each other so quickly that nobody else can understand. We speak over each other constantly, but somehow that is exactly right for us and we all enjoy it. I am not insisting you should go out and make friends with ADHDers, but knowing people with a shared lived experience is an important way of accessing information, and seeing what you might learn from them.

You can apply the techniques in this book to friendships too. If being late all the time annoys a friend, then you can employ practices to ensure you're on time, or suggest to them ideas which remove the need to be on time, such as always meeting with other friends, so if you arrive late they're not alone.

It feels frustrating to say this, but we often have to think of our friendships and relationships in the language of access too. Running on auto-pilot and hoping for the best often won't work well for relationships. We all generally accept that we have to put work into friendships, but we also need to recognise that some of that work might need to go into access too.

Romantic/sexual relationships can be equally as challenging. The world often tells us a specific story of relationships, but often this story is incompatible with ADHDers. There is no guide as to how to do this, but it's the area where I have found the ride of ADHD on TikTok most useful.

In the same way that you might need affection from your partner, ADHDers might need other less common things too. I find it strangely comforting when my partner always knows where I have left my keys. Seeing people online talk about how they manage relationships has been incredibly useful for me, and this is an area where community learning can't be underestimated.

Sometimes we also have to look into areas we might not be great at talking about. We have to consider the role of distractibility during sex, how body doubling might help with the cleaning, or how a varying love of sensory input might mean we need to navigate personal intimacy differently.

I generally find my creativity thrives when my personal life is not in crisis in some way. It doesn't matter how many access needs are being met in my creative life, if I spend all day feeling guilty because I unwittingly annoyed a friend, I won't get anything done.

TL;DR: We have to apply access methods to our friendships and relationships, and although this can be hard to navigate it can have a positive impact on our creativity.

3.8. The ADHD meltdown strategy

Even with all the advice in the world, you will still end up in difficult situations. It happens to me all the time. Halfway through making *Self-care, or...* I had a meltdown and almost gave up.

There will be intense, somewhat brief moments of frustration. I call these meltdowns. They usually occur for me when I have been working incredibly fast, or on a number of different things, and the tasks in front of me have become so overwhelming that I cannot do any of them. It feels a bit like my brain is not just trying to do all of my tasks at once, but all of the tasks in the world at once, and it is jumping between all of them.

The ideal scenario in this situation is that I drop everything and go and calm down, but unless there is someone who knows how to help me do that, then adding the task of calming down just makes it worse.

I began to develop a set routine that is written down on my phone, so I always have it with me. I do this routine regardless of anything else. For me it goes like this:

1. If there is a quieter place within eyesight of where I currently am, I go there. Otherwise, I stay where I am.

2. I close my laptop and any other device that creates overly stimulating distractions.

3. I then write down anything that I need to do in the next hour. This is often frantic and exhausts me, but that's partially the point. It's important that it is only the next hour, no longer.

4. I turn to a new piece of paper, and I write down the same list again of things I need to do in the next hour. However, I don't look at the old list, and I am aiming to reduce the number of things on the list.

5. Sometimes I will do this a third time; anything I forget is in fact not that urgent.

6. This generally gets me a list that I can put in priotity order for the next hour, and can follow.

7. Sometimes within that hour I calm down enough to break the cycle and go and do something else. Or I get to the end of the hour, and I do all the exercises again.

8. The focus is to regain a feeling of control over everything, and often the exhaustion of a meltdown means I need a nap or some kind of decompression afterwards.

When my brain reaches the point where there are hundreds of tasks and priorities in my head, I have to externalise these priorities. I can't see what's in my head and sort through the tasks, but I can see what's on paper and sort them into something more manageable.

This method might not work for everyone; some people might need to put all the tasks on Post-it notes. Some people might need someone to come and talk them through what is happening. Some people might need to go and disappear under a weighted blanket. Some people might need something entirely different.

Whatever it is, pre-plan your meltdown strategy. Make sure you've prepared a linear series of actions that can be done without having to make any big choices.

TL;DR: You need to pre-plan your meltdown strategy, because you won't be able to come up with one when it happens.

3.9. Forgetting things

A writer I hugely respect was once developing a play with one of the organisations where I had a survival job. I did everything I could to make sure I could be in the room, to learn from that writer. Then, on the first day of the workshops in a prestigious building, I arrived late. I could see the disappointment and lack of surprise from the director.

I had tried to leave the house, but couldn't find three items. This happens a lot to me, and often to other people with ADHD. Most humans have something called 'object permanence', but ADHDers don't always have an effective version of it. It means that when you put something down, you still remember it exists. But for us, when we stop interacting with something, it often ceases to exist.

This means when I put down my house keys, I don't really have much recollection of where they last were, and sometimes don't even realise they are not in my pocket. This means leaving the house in the morning is one of the most difficult parts of my day. I would try to leave but everything from my keys to my laptop would be missing. Sometimes I would get halfway to work, think of a task I needed to do later that day, look in my bag and realise I hadn't brought my laptop to do it, so I would have to go back.

It feels like a simple thing, the act of forgetting. But it's something I have very little control over, and it is probably the part of ADHD that most often causes me to have a meltdown. As soon as I have a meltdown, it's unlikely I am going to be able to do my creative practice, so it is one of the key things I have tried to deal with.

There are some really obvious, practical things that I have put in place:

1. Keys are always left in the same place by the door, so I see them as I leave and pick them up.

2. Everything for the next day must be in my bag before I go to sleep; there can be no morning packing.

3. I have cheap little GPS tags that I put on my important items, including my cat, in case I do lose them.

4. I have two of every charger I need: one that lives at home, and one that goes in my bag. I also have spare laptop chargers at home, because no matter what I do, my charger will end up left in a random building without me realising.

These are quite straightforward, practical things we can probably think of ourselves. The slightly more challenging part might be working with other people and how our forgetfulness impacts them. As I began thinking about this, it brought up two things.

Firstly, it's important to communicate to people what is happening. I felt an incredible amount of shame when I forgot things, because of the simplicity of the task. I think there's a general belief in people that the more important something is, then the easier it is to remember. This is not true for me. This means it can affect my relationships with my collaborators, commissioners and other people in my creative life. With all the ways I try and remember things, I still forget sometimes; there is no magical solution.

This is why when I have a verbal access rider chat with a new collaborator of any kind, it is one of the first things I explain to them. If I am responsible for managing their reaction to me losing things, then the shame it causes does not allow me to collaborate effectively. I do make it clear that I am doing everything in my power to remember, but it's sometimes not effective.

There is often a belief that the function of access is to make the problem disappear, but sometimes my access needs look like needing people to hold space for the mistakes that will happen, and adjust accordingly. This is one of the most difficult things to ask for in the creative industries, where often companies are managing tight budgets, but it can be the most impactful.

The second element I want to explore about memory, is that I forget things exist a lot – and people are also things. I will temporarily lose track of the existence of friends and family, and it's something I think I'll always be upset about. It means I am bad at calling my parents regularly, I'm bad at remembering to organise something with a friend, and I'm bad at remembering to text my partner when I need to.

There have been so many scenarios when I have posted on social media and said things like 'Do I know anyone who can do some photography for something?', and a friend I've known for over ten years will text me, amazed at how I didn't think about them. The truth is I couldn't think about them; I don't have a list of people readily available to search in my head. I wish I did.

It is an intense source of stress that once people disappear from my immediate present, I don't necessarily forget them, but they get a bit lost in my brain. They cease to exist in my immediate present, which is the only thing I am comprehending most of the time.

This has caused a lot of problems over the years, especially in lockdown, when I found it near impossible to keep up friendships with people remotely because my brain couldn't compute their absence.

It can make people feel very rejected, and the best way I have found to approach this is to say 'yes' where possible. If someone feels rejected, then our instinct is to say it's not our fault, it's ADHD. But it's important we validate their feelings: they did feel rejected and that is real.

Once we have said yes to this, then we might move into the 'Yes *and*…' phase, such as 'Yes, I see that, *and* I just want you to know it wasn't my intention…' The word 'but' is often a really ineffective word in emotional communication.

If we lean into it further, that's when we can finally have a conversation about how we can make sure each other's emotional needs are met. With some friends we agree that we hang out on a regular schedule which is in the diary. Almost exclusively, I only follow good friends on Instagram so I get a periodic visual reminder of them. I often use my dump list to remember that I need to arrange to hang out with them at some point.

I have a reminder that goes off every two weeks to check if I have rung my parents recently. Generally, they know they need to ring me, not out of my lack of care but because I can never remember how long it is since we last spoke. They put in this work, but generally I try not to lump all the effort on my friends and family.

The solutions are inelegant and often specific to certain situations, but this work is important work.

Forgetting things or people has often created levels of overwhelm that have derailed writing for over a week, because it has the potential to cause so much hurt in others and anger in me.

TL;DR: You forget people as well as things, and this can take the energy that you need for your creative practice.

3.10. Survival jobs

The reality of trying to have and sustain your creative practice is that income streams aren't always stable or sufficient. In theatre especially, we are seeing a further decline in secure and regular work for creatives, so that even established creatives are having to find work in related industries or outside creative sectors altogether.

I have changed roles in survival jobs about once every nine months, which is a pretty long time for someone with ADHD in my experience. Here's that journey and what I learned from each job I have done:

1. I did Front of House in West End theatres for a while. I really loved this job. I worked at the Apollo Victoria where *Wicked* is currently playing, and it was like finding a whole second family in London. I was twenty-one at the time and the social side of the job was the thing I needed to bed into London. However, the contract was incredibly casual and had varying hours every week. There was a general understanding that you worked all eight shows per week, or you got whatever shifts were left. Though Front of House work is flexible in theory, this is not necessarily the reality at bigger theatres. I was travelling to central London for shifts of about four hours, six times per week. The travel alone was costing me a lot of time that I would have preferred to spend on my creative work. If I had a workshop or a rehearsal, it was difficult to get time off at short notice, and the pay of early-career creative work isn't normally high enough to justify taking time off frequently.

2. Then I became a supervisor in the same chain of theatres. I wasn't in charge of shifts, but generally we looked after a level of the theatre each. This went part-way to solving the problem of pay because the rate was higher, and I worked longer shifts to set up and close down the theatre, so that suited me better. The shifts being longer also meant that we only worked five days per week so I often had a weekday where I could see a

show, or have meetings, or go to a workshop. ADHD means I love being under pressure, so managing fire drills and large, chaotic environments suited me fine. There is a phenomenon with ADHD where we often manage a crisis into existence, because then our brain floods with adrenaline and that is a stimulant, so it gives us focus. It's like a form of self-medication and working in a huge West End theatre definitely creates that environment. The problem was that I would have different days off on different weeks, and often finish at about 11.30 at night, and the lack of a schedule began to take its toll. Though flexibility is useful, I wasn't in control of that flexibility, so I had to expend a lot of effort to make sure I was managing my diary well and my sleep schedule was constantly in flux.

3. To combat this, I became the administrator at the theatre instead. This was my first time on a regular daily schedule, and it was not great for my flexibility, but it was great for having a regular sleep schedule and generally being organised. Arriving at work at the same time every day was useful, and as I became more experienced in the role and had things running smoothly, my manager became more comfortable with letting me change my hours when I needed to come in late or leave early for meetings. I would use holiday days for workshops and when you get a salary, your holiday days are still paid as long as you don't go over your allowance of annual leave. I accepted that slightly beige and regular work with sustained predictable income gave me a sense of stability that was incredibly useful. Yes, I had lost some flexibility, but as a writer, I didn't need to be in rehearsals as much as an actor, so I could just about make it work. The problem was that the work was pretty boring, I wasn't really doing anything creative at all and I was still working in theatre, so the pay, although stable, wasn't that good. We often feel drawn to survival jobs in theatre organisations because we have proximity to the art we want to make, but this can cause more stress due to the lower rates of pay.

4. When another admin job with a less fancy title, but much better
    pay came up – I jumped at the chance. I was the Operations
    Assistant at a theatre company called Out of Joint, but which
    changed its name to Stockroom. I could do everything they
    needed; the role was partly analytical, but I got to go to readings
    and see the shows they were making too. Though it was a culture
    shock coming from a very organised commercial theatre to a
    smaller and more stretched subsidised company, I loved it. I also
    had one of the best managers I have ever had; her name was
    Kate and I think she probably knew me better than I knew myself.
    I can't say I was always the model employee, but I think I learned
    more about managing and caring for people from her than I have
    at any other point in my life. The problem with this role was
    that I was supposed to be the first in and the last out, to unlock
    and close the building, and that requirement for someone who
    doesn't have a great grasp of time management didn't really work
    well. I would not recommend taking on a role that is supposed to
    be the point of dependability within the company.

5. At the company they needed some extra work in producing, so
    I began to help out a bit. I liked producing because it was more
    varied and closer to the art. It also gave me some capacity
    to not be the dependable person who had to be there early
    and leave later. This tendency to slip between different roles
    has been a feature of my survival jobs, because as soon as
    I put a system in place to make something work well, I began
    to get bored of running the system. As soon as I could do
    the bookkeeping at a pretty good speed, it wasn't new and
    interesting, and I lost focus. Producing, on the other hand, has
    a level of variety. I loved being the assistant producer, but as
    always, another challenge came along.

6. I applied to be on the Arts Fundraising and Philanthropy
    Fellowship (AFP) , a sort of training programme for fundraisers.
    Alongside my job I had successfully funded my own creative

projects on a fairly regular basis, and I thought that learning more about fundraising would be the most useful thing for my creativity at that point. Though this wasn't a paid job, I think there's something important I realised through this course. Though it feels important to have proximity to the art you want to do, because you think you will learn something, it's probably more important to consider the skills your creativity needs, and go and get those skills in whatever environment you can.

7. And so I became a fundraiser. Fundraising is both an analytical, structured and long-term job which doesn't often push you into irregular hours or high-stress situations that motivate but drain you. But it is also incredibly creative and benefits from the ability to tell a good story. Through understanding how money moves around the sector, I have learnt a lot about the kinds of relationships and connections I need to make to get my creative projects off the ground.

8. After a few different roles I went freelance. People often say that people with ADHD are drawn to freelance life, but I avoided it at all costs for a while. I wanted my day job to be steady and dependable, so my creative life could be more unpredictable. Being freelance with ADHD is hard, because although having a line manager who is not understanding can be challenging, the act of being in a company does almost serve a support worker function. I was in an office and without knowing it (pre-diagnosis) was able to create body-doubling situations, there was a company calendar managing my time, and people managing me to make sure I got stuff done. I was lucky to have an incredibly perceptive manager, but this isn't true for everyone.

9. Now I split my time between working freelance contracts and delivering consultancy in fundraising and development – and writing. I can control my own hours, and work in a flexible way to allow for my writing work to take place too. Good fundraisers are in high demand right now, and so my

fundraising income can cover the income I might not receive while writing. Ultimately, I am using my storytelling skills in a way that I don't think of it as a survival job any more. The work I do in fundraising feels like I am supporting projects and organisations to achieve the same thing I am trying to achieve in my writing. This arrangement is the thing that has also allowed me to become the chair of Graeae Theatre Company, join the London Area Council of ACE, and work even more expansively in cultural policy. I can't stress how important it is that you find the right arrangement to generate resources if you are not doing your creative practice full time.

From this journey I have tried to distil some principles for survival work that are important.

1. **Don't be afraid of money**: If your art doesn't pay you well, then something needs to. Often we choose survival jobs for the love, but I would challenge that and say that the more financial stability you have, the more capacity you will have to look after yourself and manage your chaotic focus.

2. **Don't feel like you have to freelance too early**: The fact that I worked for other people, and was lucky enough to find a supportive and incredible manager for about three years, meant that I developed skills which meant when I went freelance I could depend on regular work.

3. **It is not a race**: Spending all that time getting skills, as opposed to trying to get the best job title possible quickly, has been invaluable. Sure, I used to feel a bit left behind when my friends had survival jobs with more impressive job titles, but now I've been able to craft a practice which is useful for me.

4. **The boring schedule can be useful**: As much as we are often drawn to variety and chaos, this doesn't have to be reflected in our schedule. Having varied work within a predictable schedule allows me to better manage sleep and all of my other needs.

5. **You might get an alter ego**: I found it helpful for a long time to recognise that sometimes I was being writer-Tom and sometimes fundraiser-Tom. It meant I could leave behind one version of me, and go and do my creative practice. When I was focusing on making money as fundraiser-Tom, I could leave that behind and not let it blend into the practice of writer-Tom. I have two separate emails, separate websites/ online presences, so I can step between these identities. I have separate phone numbers too, so I really can 'leave the office' and not think about my survival work.

6. **Your day job might not be creative**: The role of your survival job is to create the environment you need for your creative practice to be as well-resourced as possible. If you happen to be incredibly good at coding and can get paid a lot of money for this, then you could work a few days per week to give you the resources for your creative practice the rest of the week. I know people who are doctors who work around acting.

7. **Tell people about ADHD**: Out of any environment, your survival job is the place you should talk about your ADHD. You want to remove as many barriers as possible, and having people around you that understand and can make accommodations helps you conserve energy for your creative practice.

These principles help me to commit to my creative work when I am working on it, and not worry about my income as much because I have that secured by my survival job.

This shouldn't be a choice we have to make. Creative work should have a level of stability like other careers, but we have to learn to live within the world while also changing it.

I think it's important to recognise that although people with ADHD are drawn to the creative industries because the work is interesting and varied, and more hunter-like than most other sectors – the business reality of these sectors isn't always compatible with us.

When both versions of our work are forcing us into burnout due to being under-resourced, that's doing nothing for us. If one side of ourself is generating resources to feed the other, that's when I find I thrive the most.

TL;DR: Survival jobs should help your creative self thrive, not burn you out from another side.

3.11. Emotional dysregulation and the Circles of Influence

While making *Self-care, or, how to start a revolution*, I tried so many common wellbeing practices. When I eventually made the show I had discounted most of them as pointless, but there were two that stuck in their intended form. As we performed that show, it is these two techniques I brought with me.

The first of these was an exercise called the 'Circles of Influence' which is not something I invented, but something I found online which was heavily recommended. I think it's a therapy technique though I use it in a much less formal way, as a writing exercise to regain control. It's a useful tool when you feel anxious, or emotionally dysregulated, to better understand what you are/are not in control of.

When my brain is racing and I am struggling to prioritise between certain tasks, this is often the last exercise I use to avoid hitting a meltdown moment.

The process goes like this:

1. Draw three circles on a piece of paper. These are the Circles of 'Control', 'Influence' and 'Concern'. Usually they go inside each other, but they can be beside each other, they can be boxes or triangles, I am not sure it really matters. See page 149 for an example of how you might lay it out.

2. As your thoughts race, you should externalise them and write them down in the appropriate circle. Usually, I try to write down everything that comes to mind that fits in the Circle of Control first, as it is calming. The following points explain each of the circles:

3. Anything in the Circle of Control is something you can directly control. These are things like the temperature of the room you are in or a piece of work you need to get done.

4. Anything in the Circle of Influence is something that you can influence, but not entirely control on your own. It might be something like the expectation of a colleague, that you can't control unless you have a conversation and they agree to change something.

5. Anything in the Circle of Concern, is something that concerns you, but you don't have a tangible way to do anything about it right now. This might include big things like the impending doom of climate change, but it also might include the actions of another person that you can't stop.

6. Once I've written everything down, I normally change pen colours or take a quick break and get a new piece of paper. I think the key here is that it feels like you're having a conversation with your earlier self. Generally the act of writing all of that down is somewhat calming, and you can move forwards.

7. Then the aim is to list the actions that need to be taken to make the things in the Circle of Control go away, or be quiet. If they're in the right circle then you should be in control of these things.

8. I usually aim to write actions related to about 80% of the things in the Circle of Influence. You can try and write the actions you need to take to begin influencing something, like having an initial conversation with someone. I find that generally I don't always have the capacity to deal with all of these things, which is why I aim for 80%.

9. Then finally, the most challenging thing is that you need to accept the things in the Circle of Concern are out of your control. You can't write actions to make them disappear, but I generally find I can write actions to make peace with them. For example, when I am worrying extensively about money in general, I can at least check my budget spreadsheet to know I will get to the end of the month. Or I can share that worry with someone.

10. After that, you can then choose to prioritise and action the things you've listed, using the prioritisation techniques discussed in other parts of this book.

Some adaptation and allowances I have gathered out of practice that relate to ADHD are:

1. There is a knack to figuring out what circle some things go in. Often when our mind races and because we have been socially conditioned to believe we might be a burden, we want to take responsibility for lots of things. If you can, try and really look hard for the things you can push to the last circle; there will be more than you think.

2. Body doubling while you do this is incredibly helpful, as it can make sure you don't get distracted or go off on a tangent.

3. I find there are things in the other circles that repeat a lot, that are related to my ADHD. These are things like worrying about being late to something, and I have a list on my phone of these common things. This serves as a useful reminder of things I can do to soothe worries that are common.

4. Instead of using the word 'worry', you might find it useful to use the word 'distraction'. This is a really great exercise when you feel particularly distracted, and you want to figure out which ones you can make go away. Some of the actions and strategies in the inner circle might be things found in this book.

5. The problem of our brains working quicker than we can write comes up here again, so it might be easier to find other ways of doing it. Maybe you want to record each circle into some kind of speech-to-text program or do the exercise with a support worker or friend who can help you. This can also be a helpful way of giving a worried friend a tangible way of supporting you that doesn't feel too taxing or involved.

There are lots of variations of this exercise, but it's useful to return my brain to a place where I have the agency to at least try to focus on my creative work. We underestimate how much real life impacts our ability to find the capacity for creativity; this applies to most people, but especially for ADHDers.

TL;DR: When you're feeling particularly distracted and your brain is racing, use the Circles of Influence to regain a sense of control.

3.12. Daily Pages

The second exercise I found genuinely useful, was something I had tried so many times in life and rejected. Daily Pages feels like it can only be done if your stationery is perfectly aligned in millennial pink and artfully photographed on Instagram. I feel like it has been fed into my mind by my algorithm for so long, but every time I have tried it I have just lost the notebook or forgotten to do it.

If you have managed to escape it, Daily Pages is where you free-write a stream of consciousness for a page every day. It is often described with a level of discipline and neatness which has put me off. Some people do it every day when they first wake up in the morning, before they've had coffee, medication or any kind of mechanism for making us feel vaguely human.

The thing is, I do have my own informal version of daily pages. When I feel overwhelmed, I often write a stream of consciousness. I learned at an early age that externalising my racing thoughts was just about the only way to manage them. When things are racing in my head they are an invisible ball of chaos, but on paper, I can respond to them and do something about them. I suspect this is part of the reason I became a writer. I think I'm trying to work out things in writing that I can't tangibly grasp in my head because of the relative chaos in there.

Naming things has always given them power for me, and so I named this practice 'Pages' like the practice of Daily Pages I had rejected so much. I am bad at doing something every day, I find it more manageable to set myself a target that has space for failure. At first, I decided I would try and turn this reactive Pages practice into something that happened once per week.

Generally, this was achievable, because I feel a bit overwhelmed at least once a week, so I was going to do it anyway. The sense of success after hitting the target also spurred me on to increase it.

Eventually I made it to doing Pages three times every week. The agreement I have with myself is that six days each week, I either go for a walk or do Pages; this gives me a choice and agency so I can choose the things that I need on that day. It also gives me a day to fail at that if I need to.

Pages takes practice. It is hard to write honestly at first, especially for me, since I received a late diagnosis of something which is a big part of how my brain works. I am still undoing the subconscious coping mechanisms I unknowingly developed when I was younger. Writing without these coping mechanisms, without quieting the difficult part of my brain, takes practice.

But the result is not only something that helps you externalise your thoughts, but it is something that helps you build a more honest relationship with your thoughts. My ability to employ a lot of the techniques I have found in this book comes from the way I have worked through the personal barriers to implementing them during my Pages sessions. Finding an honesty about how I feel able to use the word 'disabled' has allowed me to move past that reluctance and use the word. Finding honesty about my reluctance to have a support worker helped me have a conversation with myself about those feelings. Then, eventually, that honesty helped me have more confident conversations with other people about my needs.

Pages might not work for everyone. It might be that you would benefit from sound recording the practice, or doing it in a different way. But experimenting with how it might work for you might give you a new exercise which is incredibly useful.

TL;DR: Pages doesn't have to happen every day – make an agreement with yourself that allows for failure.

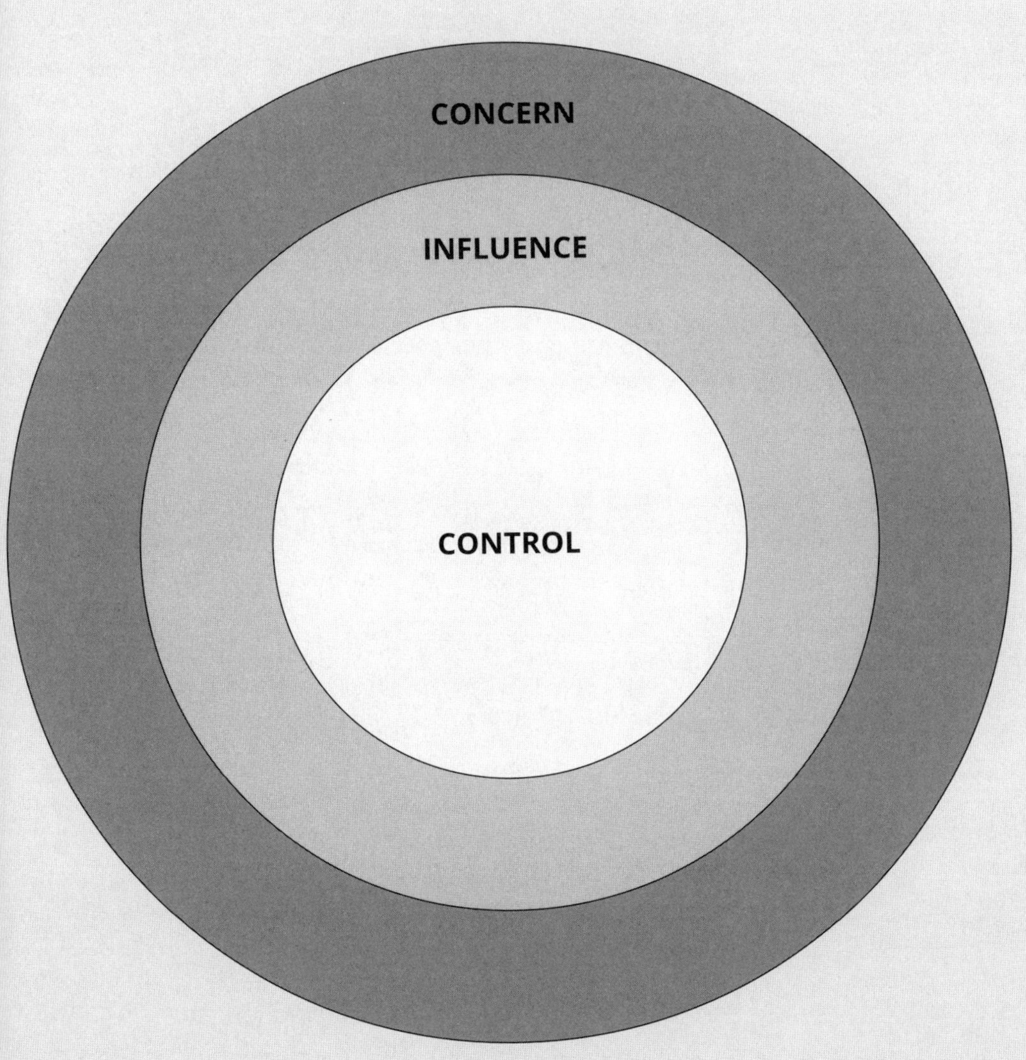

CONCERN
INFLUENCE
CONTROL

The first thing to say is that I made all the work I described in the first three parts of this book. I did the research project, I finished the Starting Blocks programme, and I made *Self-care, or, how to start a revolution*. I got to the end of them and I kept all the diaries I wrote as I was doing it.

In some way those diaries have helped me sort through the chaos of my brain that I described at the beginning of this book. As they became this book, it has brought even more comfort and order to things, as I now have a handy reference guide to remember the techniques.

But I am conflicted about this book. On the one hand, it is useful to help people manage ADHD; on the other hand, I wish it were more of a book about how we might change the world. Instead it is that last show I made: it is both self-care, and a guide to starting a revolution (I hope).

But not everything is perfect. There is no neat ending, and I don't want to promise you there is. So I have a few more things to share to prepare you for that.

4.1. You will get bored of these techniques

This book is true for me now, but in all honesty it might not be true for me in a year's time. Currently I like to use one system of task management for my writing, but at some point I might get bored of that, and I might need to invent another one.

Sometimes I cycle between using different techniques from this book, because the variety keeps me interested.

I wish this wasn't true, but it's a fundamental part of why this is not a one-size-fits-all book.

The management of ADHD requires endless creativity and imagination, to find new solutions to problems we have already solved in three different ways before.

If I find one technique starting to get boring, I actively begin looking for a new solution so that I am prepared when the old one finally stops being interesting to me.

4.2. Some things don't work

Sometimes you will try things, including things in this book, and they will not work. ADHD is not a precise or simple thing. It has variation and often interacts with other life experiences, neurodivergence and parts of our identity to make some things more challenging than others.

For example, I particularly struggle with hearing voices in loud environments and audio processing. If you play notes on a piano for me, I can hear the pitch really well. But I can't listen to a piano and sing, I can't process the audio of a piano and my own voice and compare them quickly enough to keep in tune. Anecdotally my doctor has said this is something she hears often from people with

ADHD and a history of epilepsy. But there is not enough research for her to give me an exact answer on what is happening.

If anyone ever promises you that they have a secret which is going to solve everything in your life, treat them with suspicion. ADHD does not have a secret at the end of the rainbow; it is a lifelong adventure of constant change and discovery.

That can be daunting and seem exhausting, and the reality is that it is. I sometimes wake up and want to scream with frustration, because I know I have had slightly too little sleep and my system will not be as effective that day. But I think that flexible systems can also make life full of incredible creativity too.

4.3. And what now?

If you've made it this far or skipped straight to the end, then well done. I hope this is not the end of any learning you are doing, but the beginning of a bigger exploration.

Whereas some books have very clever answers, the lack of research with ADHD means we can't make any assumptions. I have relied on building knowledge through community-sharing and pulling those different experiences into one place. Often community knowledge-sharing is the most effective method we have, and this can look like anything, from an ADHD talking group to ADHD on TikTok.

We have to critically assess the information we're receiving, and feel confident to say when something is not right for us, but we also have to be open to making discoveries in new ways that other people frown upon.

I have not been able to give you a magic solution, but if I have one final technique to leave you with, it's this:

The world encourages us to find techniques so we are less of a problem. Often this becomes known to us in the language of 'self-care' or 'access'.

But structures in the world are the things creating the problem, so they are the things that should change. Yes, this is hard work, but so is getting out of bed or remembering to eat sometimes.

Techniques to manage ADHD don't always stop the problem existing in the first place. It might be that the quickest route to peace or comfort is not to solely focus on self-care, but instead to head straight for the revolution.

Or at least, we have to survive long enough in this way of living, until we can create the right conditions to make the big change happen.

TL;DR: When something is challenging, find a solution to it, but also ask 'How can we make it so it's not like this next time?'

Extra Stuff

Normally in a book like this there is a section called Further Reading. It's normally the section I skip, because once I've read a whole book, I generally want to move on to something else. However, some people might find this useful. I've called it Extra Stuff – because it's not all about reading. In fact, some of it is actively about *avoiding* reading.

Our knowledge about ADHD is rapidly changing, and some of the resources I recommend might change or become outdated quite quickly. You might also want to go in search of your own resources. In the event that either of these things happen, I think there's three important things we should remember about content we find about ADHD:

1. You don't need to accept everything you read/hear/see. Someone might say/write something that you think doesn't apply to you. That is okay. Not all ADHDers are the same.

2. We often make impulse purchases, and some people might want to take advantage of this, selling exciting 'solutions' or tools for ADHD. It might be useful for you to check in with someone before you spend money.

3. Some of the traits you experience do relate to ADHD, but they may also relate to other things as well. There can be multiple roots of a certain behaviour; humans are complicated. Understanding your experience of ADHD might only be part of your self-awareness, and often content does not remind us of this.

Here are things I have found useful for more than a week:

If you're looking for a really broad base of suggestions of possible resources that gets updated regularly, check out the ADHD UK resources page: **adhduk.co.uk/adhd-useful-resources**

If you're interested in the book I talk about in Part Two that helped me understand the history of ADHD, you can find out more about it here: **drummerandthegreatmountain.com**

If you're looking for a browser-based timer to do body-doubling sessions with other people, have a look at Cuckoo: **cuckoo.team**

If you're interested in connecting to the wider community of disabled creatives, there's an organisation called Disability Arts Online: **disabilityarts.online/about**

If you're looking for a disabled-led radio show that often has content about ADHD, check out Access All: **bbc.co.uk/programmes/p02r6yqw**

If you're looking for something lighter which has helpful ADHD articles, there's an ADHD online magazine: **additudemag.com**

If you want to see some art made by disabled artists, there's a whole organisation dedicated to commissioning disabled artists: **weareunlimited.org.uk**

Acknowledgements

I want to acknowledge how many people it took to make sure
I actually finished this book.

To start with I want to thank all of those people and organisations
who supported me to make the shows I talk about in the book.
I cannot think of a theatre that does more to support early-career
artists than Camden People's Theatre. They gave me a second
chance at a point when I felt lost. CRIPtic have my thanks for
relentlessly building pathways for disabled artists to make work in
a landscape that is increasingly hostile. Buy tickets to their shows,
donate to their campaigns, volunteer on their boards. There will not
be a new generation of creatives without their tireless work.

This book started off as a research project I did thanks to a
Developing Your Creative Practice grant from Arts Council England.
I am hugely grateful for the time they gave me with that grant, and
I hope this book is a demonstration of the impact that can only be
achieved by giving grants to independent creatives.

Adam, I never would have considered turning that research into
a book unless you told me to and put it in front of Nick Hern
Books. I am grateful that you were an incredibly caring agent, and
endlessly enthusiastic about my work.

There are lots of artists and creatives I spoke to while making this
book, and most of them have been anonymised because they didn't
sign up to have their life shared in a book. I am hugely grateful to
everyone I spoke to, who shared their wisdom and experience with
me. I hope you see yourself in these pages.

Jane Fallowfield, I have just realised I didn't reply to your last WhatsApp, so I should do that. Also, your perceptive and caring editing of the first draft of this book was hugely instrumental in how it turned out. You listened to me ramble about it for a long time. You are more brilliant than I could put into words.

To Matt and the team at NHB, I am so sorry for my awful use of punctuation and the number of typos. You have endlessly checked details which my brain could not keep track of and championed the ideas in this book. Thank you for your patience and diligence.

To the friends and colleagues who read bits or all of this book, thank you for telling me which bits were shit, and to keep going anyway. I couldn't have made it to this point without you.

Russell T Davies, we have not met yet, but I am dying to write an episode of *Doctor Who*, so while this book is going to print, I thought I would shoot my shot.

Tom Ryalls
London, 2026